THE FALL OF SATAN

THE FALL OF SATAN

Rebels in the Garden

Bodie Hodge

First Printing: March 2011
Second printing: September 2011

Copyright © 2011 by Bodie Hodge. No part of this book may be used
or reproduced in any manner whatsoever without written permission
of the publisher, except in the case of brief quotations in articles and
reviews. For information write:
    Master Books®, P.O. Box 726, Green Forest, AR 72638
Master Books® is a division of the New Leaf Publishing Group, Inc.

ISBN: 978-0-89051-606-5
Library of Congress Number: 2011920854

Unless otherwise noted, all Scripture is taken from the NKJV (New King
James Version, copyright © 1982 by Thomas Nelson, Inc. Used by
permission. All rights reserved). Scripture in chapter 35 is from the
NASB (New American Standard Bible®, copyright ©1960, 1962, 1963,
1968, 1971, 1972, 1973, 1975, 1977, 1995 by the Lockman Foundation.
Used by permission).

Please consider requesting that a copy of this volume be purchased by
your local library system.

Printed in the United States of America

Please visit our website for other great titles:
www.masterbooks.net

For information regarding author interviews,
please contact the publicity department at (870) 438-5288.

Master Books®
A Division of New Leaf Publishing Group
www.masterbooks.net

Acknowledgments

Special thanks to the many reviewers and editors for chapters included in this book: Steve Fazekas, Dr. Terry Mortenson, Dr. Andrew Snelling, David Jolly, David Wright, Gary Vaterlaus, Stacia McKeever, Dr. Jason Lisle, Dr. Tommy Mitchell, Frost Smith, Tim Chaffey, Erik Lutz, Jeremy Ham, Donna O'Daniel, Dr. Georgia Purdom, John Upchurch, Lori Jaworski, Paul F. Taylor, and Ken Ham.

Also a special thanks to Professor Andy McIntosh for his contribution to the chapter on defense/attack structures, which is reprinted from *The New Answers Book* and to Dan Lietha for providing the bulk of the artwork.

Contents

Foreword

"... lest Satan should take advantage of us; for we are not ignorant of his devices" (2 Corinthians 2:11).

The reality of Satan and his work, specifically in the Garden of Eden, has spawned numerous questions that Christians have been struggling to answer. In a scientific age, many Christians wonder if Genesis can even be trusted. Often, they simply avoid these questions. But should we as Christians shy away from answering? Absolutely not, for we are not ignorant of Satan's devices.

Some of the most common questions asked at Answers in Genesis and to the church as a whole, *next to evolution and millions of years*, relate to Satan, the origin of sin and evil, and the Fall of man in general.[1] On average, the ministry receives about five to ten questions per week on this topic alone! So there was a real need to get these answers out as well.

To be answered properly, many questions *must* go back to the Curse in Genesis 3 and other early chapters in Genesis. This is exactly what Bodie Hodge has done as he dives into the Scriptures to answer some tough questions. Such questions are having an impact, but few realize how important these questions are. They are, in fact, the very foundation for the Gospel. It was the Fall of man (Adam and Eve) that put us into a bind ... that required a Savior — Jesus Christ.

Satan and the origin of evil are hot topics in today's culture because the world is attacking the reality of Satan and claiming that evil doesn't even exist. And the Church, by and large, has few *lay* biblical resources on the subject to counter such claims. Rarely do resources take questions like these back to the Curse in Genesis 3 *and* make them relevant today. Yet this book does both.

Christians can give easy-to-read, reasoned, biblical answers to help strengthen their faith and share with others. So this general apologetics book should be an excellent resource that looks closely at the bad news in Genesis but also shares the powerful good news of Jesus Christ and His sacrifice that has conquered sin, Satan, and evil once for all.

Introduction

Each question answered in this book is a genuine question that has been asked many times over. These and similar questions are valid questions to ask. To answer them, we need to carefully consider what the Bible says, since it is the only completely reliable source of information about Satan. The Bible doesn't give much information about Satan and angels, since it was written to man,[2] but it does give enough to reasonably answer some of these questions.

God's Word is infallible and the absolute authority and we need to be leery of absolute conclusions drawn from sources outside the Bible, such as man's ideas or traditions.[3]

1. Who is Satan and was he always called "Satan"?

The first use of the name *Satan* is found in 1 Chronicles 21:1; chronologically, this is surpassed by Job, which was written much earlier. *Satan* is found throughout Job chapters 1 and 2. Satan (*satan*) literally means *adversary* in Hebrew. The etymology of the name is discussed briefly by Justin Martyr, an early church father, around A.D. 156. He says:

> Or He meant the devil by the lion roaring against Him: whom Moses calls the serpent, but in Job and Zechariah he is called the devil, and by Jesus is addressed as Satan, showing that a compounded name was acquired by him from the deeds which he performed. For "Sata" in the Jewish and Syrian tongue means apostate; and "Nas" is the word from which he is called by interpretation the *serpent*, i.e., according to the interpretation of the Hebrew term, from both of which there arises the single word Satanas.[4]

Another name appears in the Old Testament in the King James Version:

> How art thou fallen from heaven, O Lucifer, son of the morning! How art thou cut down to the ground, which didst weaken the nations! (Isaiah 14:12; KJV).

This is the only passage that uses the name Lucifer to refer to Satan. This name doesn't come from Hebrew but Latin. Perhaps this translation into English was influenced by the *Latin Vulgate*, which uses this name. In Latin, Lucifer means light bringer.

The Hebrew is *heylel* and means light bearer, shining one, or morning star. Many modern translations translate this as "star of the morning" or "morning star." In this passage, *heylel* refers to the king of Babylon and Satan figuratively. Of course, Jesus lays claim to this title in Revelation 22:16. Though the passage in Revelation is in Greek while the passage in

Isaiah is Hebrew, both are translated similarly.

Some believe that Lucifer was a heavenly or angelic name that was taken from Satan when he rebelled. The Bible doesn't explicitly state this, though Satan is nowhere else referred to as Lucifer but instead is called other names like the devil, Satan, etc. This tradition may hold some truth, although the idea seems to miss that this verse is referring to him during and after his fall — not before. Since other scriptural passages refer to him as Satan, Lucifer wasn't necessarily his pre-Fall name any more than Satan would be.

Even though Satan is first mentioned by name in Job, previous historical accounts record his actions. See Genesis 3 when Satan influenced the serpent, in Genesis 4 and 1 John 3:12 where Cain belonged to him when he slew his brother, and in Revelation 12:9.

In the New Testament, other names reveal more about Satan's current nature. Devil (*diabolos*) means false accuser, Satan, and slanderer in Greek, and is the word from which the English word diabolical is formed. Satan is called dragon in Revelation 12:9 and Revelation 20:2, as well as the evil one in several places. Other names for Satan include ancient serpent/serpent of old (Revelation 12:9), Abaddon (destruction), Apollyon (destroyer) (Revelation 9:11), Beelzebub/Beelzebul (Matthew 12:27), Belial (2 Corinthians 6:15), and tempter (Matthew 4:3).

Satan is also referred to as the "god of this world/age" (2 Corinthians 4:4), "prince of this world" (John 12:31), and "father of lies" (John 8:44).

2. Was Satan originally a fallen angel from heaven?

Satan is mentioned in conjunction with angels (Matthew 25:41; Revelation 12:9) and the "sons of God" (Job 1:6, 2:1), which many believe to be angels. Although no Bible verse actually states that he was originally an angel, he is called a cherub in Ezekiel 28:16. The meaning of cherub is uncertain, though it is usually thought of as an angelic or heavenly being. (Ezekiel 28 is discussed in more detail later.)

In 2 Corinthians 11:14, we find that Satan masquerades as an angel of light — another allusion to his angel-like status:

> And no wonder! For Satan himself transforms himself into an angel of light (2 Corinthians 11:14).

Although it is possible that Satan was an angel, it may be better to say that he was originally among the "heavenly host" since he came from heaven, but we don't know with certainty that he was an actual angel (heavenly host would include angels). Recall Isaiah 14:12:

> How you are fallen from heaven, O Lucifer, son of the morning! How you are cut down to the ground, you who weakened the nations!

When Satan, the great dragon in Revelation 12:9, fell, it appears that he took a third of the heavenly host with him (a "third of the stars" were taken to earth with him by his tail, Revelation 12:4). Angels who fell have nothing good to look forward to:

> Then He will also say to those on the left hand, "Depart from Me, you cursed, into the everlasting fire prepared for the devil and his angels" (Matthew 25:41).

> For if God did not spare the angels who sinned, but cast them down to hell and delivered them into chains of darkness, to be reserved for judgment . . . (2 Peter 2:4).

What these passages *don't* say is who and where the angels and Satan were originally.

> And it grew up to the host of heaven; and it cast down some of the host and some of the stars to the ground, and trampled them (Daniel 8:10).

Daniel is speaking of heavenly hosts and angels, which were often spoken of as stars or luminaries (see Judges 5:20; Daniel 8:10; Jude 13; Revelation 1:20). It is unlikely that this passage refers to physical stars, as such would destroy the earth. The Hebrew word for stars (*kowkab*) also includes planets, meteors, and comets. Were these stars, comets, and meteors? Likely not since the context refers to heavenly beings, which would be "trampled on." This is further confirmation that Satan (and perhaps some other heavenly host) and his angels sinned and fell.

Another key passage to this is Ezekiel 28:15–17 (discussed in more detail later). The passage indicates that Satan was indeed perfect before his fall. He was in heaven and was cast to the earth.

3. Were the *heaven of heavens*, Satan, and his angels created?

The Bible doesn't give an *exact* time of Satan's creation or of his fall but does give some clues. Paul says in Colossians that *all things* were created by God/Christ:

> For by Him all things were created that are in heaven and that are on earth, visible and invisible, whether thrones or dominions or principalities or powers. All things were created through Him and for Him (Colossians 1:16).

So logically, Satan was created, as was the "heaven of heavens." Recall that Satan was originally in heaven prior to his fall. So the question becomes, when was the heaven of heavens created? The Bible uses the word *heaven* in several ways. The first mention is Genesis 1:1:

> In the beginning God created the heavens and the earth.

The Hebrew word for heavens is plural (*shamayim* dual of an unused singular *shameh*). The word itself means heaven, heavens, sky, visible heavens, abode of stars, universe, atmosphere, and the abode of God. The context helps determine the meaning of a particular word; *heavens* is properly plural, and many Bible scholars and translators have rightly translated it as such.

Therefore, it seems safe to assume that the "heaven of heavens" was created along with the physical heavens (the space-time continuum, i.e., the physical universe, where the stars, sun, and moon would abide after they were created on day 4) during creation week.

The definition of the Greek word for heaven(s) (*ouranos*) is similar: the vaulted expanse of the sky with all things visible in it; the universe, the world; the aerial heavens or sky, the region where the clouds and the tempests gather, and where thunder and lightning are produced; the sidereal or starry heavens; the region above the sidereal heavens, the seat of order of things eternal and consummately perfect where God and other heavenly beings dwells.

By usage, this could include the heaven of heavens. However, other biblical passages also help to answer whether the heaven of heavens was created.

> You alone are the LORD; You have made heaven, the heaven of heavens, with all their host, the earth and everything on it, the seas and all that is in them, and You preserve them all. The host of heaven worships You (Nehemiah 9:6).

A clear distinction is made between at least two heavens — the physical heavens and the heaven of heavens. The physical heavens include the expanse made on day 2, the place where the stars were placed on day 4, and the atmosphere (birds are referred to as "of the air" and "of the heavens," e.g., 1 Kings 14:11, Job 12:7, Psalm 104:12). The heaven of heavens is the "residing place" (if such can be said) of the heavenly host, angels, and so on. This may be the third heaven that Paul mentions:

> I know a man in Christ who fourteen years ago — whether in the body I do not know, or out of the body I do not know, God knows — such a one was caught up to the third heaven (2 Corinthians 12:2).

The passage in Nehemiah indicates that God made the heavens; they are not infinite as God is. So the question now becomes, when?

Since the heaven of heavens is referred to with the earth, seas, and physical heaven, we can safely assume that they were all created during the same time frame — during creation week. The creation of the heaven of heavens did not take place on day 7, as God rested on that day from all of His work of creating. So it must have happened sometime during the six prior days.

> Then God saw everything that He had made, and indeed it was very good. So the evening and the morning were the sixth

day. Thus the heavens and the earth, and all the host of them, were finished (Genesis 1:31–2:1).

Everything that God made, whether on earth, sky, seas, or heaven, was "very good." Did this include the heaven of heavens and Satan and the angels? Absolutely! Satan is spoken of in Ezekiel 28:15:

> You were perfect in your ways from the day you were created,
> till iniquity was found in you.

This passage says that Satan was blameless, hence he was *very good* originally. It would make sense then that the heaven of heavens was also a recipient of this blessed saying, since Satan was. In fact, this is what we would expect from an all-good God: a very good creation. Deuteronomy 32:4 says every work of God is perfect. So the heaven of heavens, Satan, and the angels were originally very good.

Ezekiel 28:15 says "from the *day*" (emphasis added) Satan was created. Obviously then, Satan had a beginning; he is not infinite as God is. Thus, Satan has some sort of binding to time. Other Scriptures also reveal the relationship between Satan and time.

> Therefore rejoice, O heavens, and you who dwell in them! Woe to the inhabitants of the earth and the sea! For the devil has come down to you, having great wrath, because he knows that he has a short time (Revelation 12:12).

> When the devil had ended every temptation, he departed from Him until an opportune time (Luke 4:13).

As a created being with a beginning, Satan is bound by time. He is not omnipresent as God is, nor is he omniscient. God has declared the end from the beginning (Isaiah 46:10); Satan cannot.

We can be certain that Satan, the heaven of heavens, and all that is in them had a beginning.

4. When were the angels and Satan created?

The Bible doesn't give the exact timing of the creation of Satan and the angels; however, several deductions can be made from Scripture concerning the timing. Consider Ezekiel 28:11–19:

Moreover the word of the LORD came to me, saying,

"Son of man, take up a lamentation for the king of Tyre, and say to him, 'Thus says the Lord GOD: "You were the seal of perfection, full of wisdom and perfect in beauty.

You were in Eden, the garden of God; every precious stone was your covering: the sardius, topaz, and diamond, beryl, onyx, and jasper, sapphire, turquoise, and emerald with gold. The workmanship of your timbrels and pipes was prepared for you on the day you were created.

You were the anointed cherub who covers; I established you; you were on the holy mountain of God; you walked back and forth in the midst of fiery stones.

You were perfect in your ways from the day you were created, till iniquity was found in you.

By the abundance of your trading you became filled with violence within, and you sinned; therefore I cast you as a profane thing out of the mountain of God; and I destroyed you, O covering cherub, from the midst of the fiery stones.

Your heart was lifted up because of your beauty; you corrupted your wisdom for the sake of your splendor; I cast you to the ground, I laid you before kings, that they might gaze at you.

You defiled your sanctuaries by the multitude of your iniquities, by the iniquity of your trading; therefore I brought fire from your midst; it devoured you, and I turned you to ashes upon the earth in the sight of all who saw you.

All who knew you among the peoples are astonished at you; you have become a horror, and shall be no more forever." ' "

In the sections prior to this, the word of the Lord was to Tyre itself (Ezekiel 27:2) and to the ruler of Tyre (Ezekiel 28:2). Beginning in Ezekiel 28:11, a lament (expression of grief or mourning for past events) is expressed to the king of Tyre; or more specifically, to the one *influencing* the king of Tyre. Note well that the king of Tyre was never a model of perfection (verse 12), nor was he on the mount of God (verse 14), nor was he in the Garden of Eden (verse 13; note that the Flood has destroyed the Garden of Eden several hundred years prior to this time period).

God easily sees Satan's influence and speaks directly to him. Elsewhere the Lord spoke to the serpent in Genesis 3 — Genesis 3:14 is said to the serpent; Genesis 3:15 is said to Satan who influenced the serpent. Jesus rebuked Peter and then spoke to Satan (Mark 8:33). In Isaiah 14, the passage speaks to the king of Babylon and some parts to Satan, who was influencing him.

In the Ezekiel passage we note that Satan was originally perfect (blameless) from the *day* he was created until he sinned (wickedness was found in him). Thus, it can be deduced that Satan was created during creation week; since he was blameless, he was under God's "very good" proclamation (Genesis 1:31) at the end of day 6.

In Job 38:4–7, God spoke to Job:

"Where were you when I laid the foundations of the earth? Tell Me, if you have understanding. Who determined its measurements? Surely you know! Or who stretched the line upon it? To what were its foundations fastened? Or who laid its cornerstone, when the morning stars sang together, and all the sons of God shouted for joy?"

Although a poetic passage, it may tell us that some of God's creative work was eyewitnessed by angels and that morning stars sang. Are morning stars symbolic of heavenly host or other angelic beings? It is possible — recall that stars are often equated with angelic or heavenly beings, and most commentators suggest this refers to angels.

If so, the creation of the angels was prior to day 3 during creation week. From Genesis 1, God created the foundations of the earth on either day 1 (earth created) or day 3 (land and water separated). The logical inference is that the angels were created on either day 1 or at least by day 3.

If not, then the physical stars (created on day 4) were present while the angels shouted for joy. If this was the case, then morning stars and angels did their singing and shouting after the stars were created.

It seems most likely that *morning stars* symbolize heavenly host or angels. Satan, one of the heavenly host, was called a morning star; therefore, Satan and the angels were created sometime prior to day 3 (or early on day 3), possibly on day 1.

5. When did Satan fall?

Satan sinned when pride overtook him and he fell from perfection (Ezekiel 28:15–17). When was this? The Bible doesn't give an exact answer but deductions can again be made from the Scriptures.

> How you are fallen from heaven, O Lucifer, son of the morning! How you are cut down to the ground, you who weakened the nations! For you have said in your heart: "I will ascend into heaven, I will exalt my throne above the stars of God; I will also sit on the mount of the congregation on the farthest sides of the north; I will ascend above the heights of the clouds, I will be like the Most High" (Isaiah 14:12–14).

When he sinned, he was cast from heaven (Isaiah 14:12). This must have been after day 6 of creation week because God pronounced everything very good (Genesis 1:31). Otherwise, God would have pronounced Satan's rebellion very good; yet throughout Scripture, God is absolute that sin is detestable in His eyes.

God sanctified the seventh day. It seems unlikely that God would have sanctified a day in which a great rebellion occurred. In Genesis 1:28, God commanded Adam and Eve to be fruitful and multiply. Had they waited very long to have sexual relations, they would have been sinning against God by not being fruitful. So it couldn't have been long after day 7 that Satan tempted the woman through the serpent.

Archbishop Ussher, the great 17th-century Bible scholar, placed Satan's fall on the tenth day of the first year, which is representative of the Day of Atonement. The Day of Atonement reflected back to the sin and sacrifice, including the first sacrifice when God made coverings for Adam and Eve from the coats of animal skins (Genesis 3:21). It may be that the generations that followed (from Abel to Noah to Abraham to the Israelites) mimicked this pattern of sacrificing for sins on the Day of

Atonement. Regardless, the fall of Satan would likely have been soon after day 7.

Some have claimed that Satan's fall was between Genesis 1:1 and Genesis 1:2. This is popularly called *gap theory*, which was popularized by Scottish theologian Thomas Chalmers in the 1800s while trying to accommodate the secular view of fossil and rock layers that the secularists claim is "millions of years" into the Bible.[5] Gap theorists try to make the case that the Hebrew in Genesis 1:2 should be translated as "And the earth *became* without form, and void" and this is subsequent to Satan's fall.

However, recognized grammarians, lexicographers, and linguists have almost uniformly rejected the translations "became" and "had become." It is a basic exegetical fallacy to claim that because *Strong's Concordance* lists "became" as one of the meanings of *haya* (Hebrew word used for "was"), it is legitimate to translate it this way in *the particular context of Genesis 1:2*. It is simply grammatically impossible when the verb *haya* is combined with a *waw* disjunctive — in the rest of the Old Testament, *waw* + a noun + *haya* (qal perfect, third person) is always translated, "was" or "came," but *never* "became."

Further, Moses also makes it very clear (e.g., Exodus 20:11, Exodus 31:17) that *all things* were created in six actual days.[6] Additionally, the idea that there were life forms that we find in the fossils that lived *and died* prior to the creation of Adam or the animals and the subsequent entrance of sin into the world undermines the gospel and denigrates the character of God.

When He was finished creating, God looked at His completed creation and called it "very good" (Genesis 1:31). Accepting "millions of years" of prior life forms living and dying (and suffering from terrible diseases such as cancer or brain tumors that we find in the fossil layers) means that God labeled this process "good." But can we honestly think death (and disease, pain, and suffering) is good?

Paul describes death as an *enemy* (1 Corinthians 15:26), and John tells us that it has no place in the new heavens and earth (Revelation 21:4). In fact, death was Adam's *punishment* for disobeying God (Genesis 2:17, Genesis 3:19, Romans 5:12). If Adam's punishment was *very good*, then why didn't he eat from the tree of knowledge of good and evil right away? And why would Jesus Christ come and die in our place to save us from death if death were a "very good" process that had been occurring for billions of years?

Millions of years of rock and fossil layers virtually disappear in light of the global Flood in Genesis 6–8, which is the cause for the bulk of the fossil and rock layers. If one accepts the fossil and rock layers as representing millions of years, then one is trusting man's ideas about the past over God's Word, which reveals the past. It is better to stand on the authority of the Word of God that doesn't change, as opposed to the changing ideas of man about the past.

Figure 1. Two ways of looking at the rock layers

Consider Jesus' words in Mark 10:6 when asked about marriage and divorce. Jesus responded:

> But from the beginning of creation, God made them male and female.

If the world really were billions of years old and man just showed up recently, then Jesus would be wrong — He should have said "*near the end of creation.*" But since the world was only about 4,000 years old when Jesus said this, and He had created man and woman on day 6 (only five days after "the beginning"), then Jesus was correct. Jesus believed in a young earth and not the "gap theory," so there is no reason for us to accept this unbiblical idea.[7]

6. How could Satan, who was created good, become evil?

From what we can tell from studying the Bible, Satan was the first to sin. He sinned before the woman sinned, and before Adam sinned. Some claim that we sin because Satan enters us and causes us to sin, but the Bible doesn't teach this. We sin whether Satan enters or not. Satan was influencing the serpent when the woman sinned and when Adam sinned; they sinned on their own accord without being able to claim that "Satan made me do it." But what caused this initial sin? Why did Satan sin in the first place?

> Let no one say when he is tempted, "I am tempted by God"; for God cannot be tempted by evil, nor does He Himself tempt anyone. But each one is tempted when he is drawn away by his own desires and enticed. Then, when desire has conceived, it gives birth to sin; and sin, when it is full-grown, brings forth death (James 1:13–15).

Death is the punishment for sin. Sin originates in desire — one's *own* desire. It was by Satan's own desire that his pride in his own beauty and abilities overtook him.

In the "very good" original creation, Satan and mankind had the power of contrite choice.[8] In the Garden of Eden, the woman was convinced by her own *desire* (the tree was *desirable* to make one wise — Genesis 3:6). Satan had not entered her; she was enticed by her own desire.

God is not the author of sin; our desires are. God did not trick or deceive Satan into becoming full of pride. God hates pride (Proverbs 8:13), and it would not be in His character to cause one to become prideful. Nor was He the one who deceived Eve. Deception and lies go hand in hand (Psalm 78:36, Proverbs 12:17), yet God does not lie or deceive (Titus 1:2, Hebrews 6:18).

Note that since Satan's *own desires* caused his pride, the blame for evil's entrance into creation cannot be attributed to God. To clarify, this doesn't mean God was unaware this would happen, but God permitted it to happen. God is sovereign and acted justly by casting Satan out of heaven using Michael and his angels after he rebelled against the Creator (Revelation 12:7–9). Therefore, when God-incarnate came to destroy evil and the work of the devil (1 John 3:8), it was truly an act of love, not a gimmick to correct what some falsely claim that He "messed up." He was glorified in His plan for redemption.

Some have asked why God didn't send Satan to hell instead of casting him to earth, assuming this would have prevented death, suffering, or curses for mankind. But God is love, and this shows that God was patient with him as God is patient with us. Perhaps Satan would have had a possibility of salvation had he not continued in his rebellion and sealed his fate, although Genesis 3:15 revealed that Satan's head would be crushed (after his continued sin and deception of the woman).

A related question is: was Satan required for man to sin? Satan's temptation of the woman instigated her to look at the fruit of the tree of the knowledge of good and evil, but it was she who *desired* it and sinned. Can we really say with certainty that on another day, without Satan, the woman and/or Adam would not have desired the fruit and sinned? However, in the words of Aslan, the lion in C.S. Lewis's *Chronicles of Narnia*, "There are no what-ifs."

In reality, we suffer death and the Curse because Adam sinned (Genesis 3) and we sinned in Adam (Hebrews 7:9–10), and we continue to sin (Romans 5:12). Adam did his part, but we must take responsibility for our part in committing high treason against the Creator of the universe. It is faulty to think that death and suffering are the result of Satan's rebellion.

Man had dominion over the world, and Satan did not (Genesis 1:26–28). When Satan rebelled, the world wasn't cursed; when Adam sinned, the ground was cursed, death entered the world, and so on. This is why we needed a last Adam (1 Corinthians 15:45), not a "last Eve" or "last Satan." This is why Christ came. The good news is that for those in Christ, the punishment for sin (death) will have no sting (1 Corinthians 15:55) and they will have eternal life.

7. Why would God, who is not evil, allow evil to continue to exist?

As with some other questions in this book, great theologians have struggled over how to effectively answer this. Paul, in his book to the Christians in Rome, offers some insight into the overarching perspective that we should have:

> And we know that all things work together for good to those who love God, to those who are the called according to His purpose (Romans 8:28).

All things, including the evil in this world, have a purpose. God is glorified through the plan of salvation that He worked out from the beginning. From the first Adam to the Last Adam, God planned a glorious way to redeem a people for Himself through the promise of a Savior who would conquer both sin and death.

Jesus was glorified when He conquered Satan, sin, and death through His death and resurrection (John 7:39, 11:4, 12:16, 12:23; Acts 3:13; 1 Peter 1:21). Both God the Son and God the Father were gloried through the Resurrection (John 11:4, 13:31–32). Everything that happens is for the glory of God, even when we can't see how God can be glorified from our limited perspective.

Jesus also gave a parable on the subject:

> Another parable He put forth to them, saying: "The kingdom of heaven is like a man who sowed good seed in his field; but while men slept, his enemy came and sowed tares among the wheat and went his way. But when the grain had sprouted and produced a crop, then the tares also appeared. So the servants of the owner came and said to him, 'Sir, did you not sow good seed in your field? How then does it have tares?' He said to them, 'An

enemy has done this.' The servants said to him, 'Do you want us then to go and gather them up?' But he said, 'No, lest while you gather up the tares you also uproot the wheat with them. Let both grow together until the harvest, and at the time of harvest I will say to the reapers, "First gather together the tares and bind them in bundles to burn them, but gather the wheat into my barn" ' " (Matthew 13:24–30).

For a short time, evil is permitted until the final "harvest." If one uproots the "tares" (non-Christians) then you may damage the "wheat" that is growing (Christians). Consider for a moment that there are Christians who come out of non-Christian families. If the non-Christians were uprooted, then so would those Christians before they would have ever been born. Those who have received the gift of eternal life look forward to the time when we join God in heaven (wheat into my barn) — a place where there will be no evil (Revelation 21:27).

This six-thousand-year-old cursed world (so far) is only a blip compared to eternity. So from the big picture, this relatively brief time that evil is permitted is not much at all.

8. What will become of Satan?

Satan's days are numbered, and he will be condemned eternally.

Therefore rejoice, O heavens, and you who dwell in them! Woe to the inhabitants of the earth and the sea! For the devil has come down to you, having great wrath, because he knows that he has a short time (Revelation 12:12).

And he cast him into the bottomless pit, and shut him up, and set a seal on him, so that he should deceive the nations no more till the thousand years were finished. But after these things he must be released for a little while (Revelation 20:3).

We should have no fear of Satan or his minions, since God has power over him and has already decreed what his outcome will be — a second death — an eternal punishment called hell.

Then He will also say to those on the left hand, "Depart from Me, you cursed, into the everlasting fire prepared for the devil and his angels" (Matthew 25:41).

The devil, who deceived them, was cast into the lake of fire and brimstone where the beast and the false prophet are. And they will be tormented day and night forever and ever (Revelation 20:10).

Then Death and Hades were cast into the lake of fire. This is the second death (Revelation 20:14).

Some people may claim that they want to "rule with Satan in hell," rather than go to heaven with and enjoy the infinite goodness of God. Sadly, these people fail to realize that Satan has *no* power in hell, nor will they. Satan is not the "ruler" in hell but a captive just as they will be if they don't receive the free gift of eternal life by repenting of their sins and believing in the finished work of Jesus Christ on the Cross.

There will be nothing good in hell — no friendships, no companionships, no love, etc. Good things come from a good God, and hell is separation from God and likewise, separation from all good things.

We trust those reading this book will realize that the only way of salvation is found through a personal saving belief in Jesus Christ. God has provided a way of salvation, a right relationship with Him, and a means of forgiveness; have you received Christ as your Savior?

9. Did the serpent originally have legs?

Perhaps one of the most-asked and most-debated topics is the serpent's original appearance. The model of the serpent here at the Answers in Genesis Creation Museum exhibit just outside of Cincinnati, Ohio, is pictured below to consider.

Determining features of the serpent from the precious little information given in the Bible is a difficult task, and there is considerable speculation in this area. For example, we can speculate about what color and patterns were on the serpent's exterior, what shape of eyes did the serpent have, and so on.

What Does the Bible Say?

Even the question of legs on the serpent is one with varying speculation. Consider the biblical text to see what it says of the serpent:

Figure 2. Serpent in the Garden of Eden at the Creation Museum.

> Now the serpent was more cunning than any beast of the field which the LORD God had made. And he said to the woman, "Has God indeed said, 'You shall not eat of every tree of the garden'?"
>
> And the woman said to the serpent, "We may eat the fruit of the trees of the garden; but of the fruit of the tree which is in the midst of the garden, God has said, 'You shall not eat it, nor shall you touch it, lest you die.'"
>
> Then the serpent said to the woman, "You will not surely die. For God knows that in the day you eat of it your eyes will be opened, and you will be like God, knowing good and evil" (Genesis 3:1–5).

> And the LORD God said to the woman, "What is this you have done?" The woman said, "The serpent deceived me, and I ate."
>
> So the LORD God said to the serpent: "Because you have done this, you are cursed more than all cattle, and more than every beast of the field; on your belly you shall go, and you shall eat dust all the days of your life. And I will put enmity between you and the woman, and between your seed and her Seed; He shall bruise your head, and you shall bruise His heel" (Genesis 3:13–15).

When looking at Genesis 3:13–15, there is no direct indication that the serpent had legs, only that its curse would be "on your belly you shall go." But in Genesis 3:1, we get a clue that the serpent was likely classified as a beast of the field, which is probably why beasts of the field were also mentioned in 3:14.[9]

What makes this an issue is that it was a *land* animal and/or flying reptile in general — hence, it moved by flying, slithering, or with append-ages. If it slithered already, what was the point of the curse and why compare it to creatures that had legs in Genesis 3:14?

Regardless if it was a beast of the field, the serpent was indeed a land animal and capable of locomotion in the Garden of Eden and in the field. Let's evaluate forms of locomotion to see the possibilities.

Locomotion

Land animals are currently known to have three classes of locomotion.[10] They are:

1. Legged (or some form of appendages)
2. Slithering
3. Rolling

Beasts of the field, and virtually all land animals, use legs to move, from cattle as a quadruped to inch worms, which use two grabbing spots on their body to inch along. Of course, snakes and legless lizards slither.

The other means of locomotion is rolling. Few creatures today roll, and of these creatures, the rolling is only temporary. The primary means is using gravity and balling up to roll down a hill, like a web-toed salamander or a Namid wheeling spider.

Few land animals have a self-powered rolling mechanism. There are two that come to mind — mother-of-pearl moth caterpillar stage and the Pangolins both use a leg(s) and/or tail with which to push. But even these rolling creatures use some form of appendage or leg; so, arguably, there are really only two types of locomotion found among animals today: slithering or legged. Was there some other form of locomotion among creatures that are now extinct? Without further research, there is no certain answer.

As for the possibility of wings, this can't be entirely ruled out either. But if so, then the serpent had some form of locomotion other than slithering and some form of appendage that physically changed forms.

Hebrew and Greek

The Hebrew word for *serpent* is *nachash*, and the Greek equivalent is *ophis*. It means "snake, serpent, sly, cunning, and image of a serpent." The late Dr. Henry Morris says of the Hebrew word:

There has been much speculation as to whether the serpent originally was able to stand upright (the Hebrew word *nachash*, some maintain, originally meant "shining, upright creature").[11]

Although this speculated meaning may have been deduced from Genesis 3:14 regarding the serpent being forced to crawl on its belly, this doesn't really help us ascertain if the serpent had legs or not.

Commentaries

Several commentaries were checked to see what other scholars said about the serpent. They are accumulated below. Of course, commentaries are not inspired like the Bible is, but they can give us some insight.

Table 1. Commentaries and the Serpent's Appearance

Commentator(s)	Legs/ physical change?	Comment(s)
1 Henry Morris[12]	Yes	"The body of the serpent, in addition, was altered even further by eliminating his ability to stand erect, eye-to-eye with man as it were." "It is further possible that all these animals (other than the birds) were quadrupeds, except the serpent, who had the remarkable ability, with a strong vertebral skeleton supported by limbs, to rear and hold himself erect when talking with Adam and Eve."
2 John Gill[13]	Yes (whether feet or flying)	"Jarchi thinks it had feet before, but were cut off on this account, and so became a reptile, as some serpents now have feet like geese, as Pliny relates; or it might go in a more erect posture on its hinder feet, as the basilisk, which is one kind of serpent, now does; and if it was a flying one, bright and shining in the air, now it should lose all its glory, and grovel in the dust, and with pain, or at least with

			pain, or at least with difficulty, creep along on its breast and belly; and this, as it respects the punishment of the devil, may signify, that he being cast down from the realms of bliss and glory, shall never be able to rise more, and regain his former place and dignity."
3	Matthew Henry[14]	Yes (perhaps feet and wings)	"He is to be for ever looked upon as a vile and despicable creature, and a proper object of scorn and contempt: *'Upon thy belly thou shalt go*, no longer upon feet, or half erect, but thou shalt crawl along, thy belly cleaving to the earth,' an expression of a very abject miserable condition."
4	John Calvin[15]	No	"This objection has induced certain men of learning and ability to say that the serpent had been accustomed to walk with an erect body before it had been abused by Satan. There will, however, be no absurdity in supposing that the serpent was again consigned to that former condition, to which he was already naturally subject. For thus he, who had exalted himself against the image of God, was to be thrust back into his proper rank; as if it had been said, 'Thou, a wretched and filthy animal, hast dared to rise up against man, whom I appointed to the dominion of the whole world; as if, truly, thou, who art fixed to the earth, hadst any right to penetrate into heaven. Therefore, I now throw thee back again to the place whence thou hast attempted to emerge, that thou mayest learn to be contented with thy lot, and no more exalt thyself, to man's reproach and injury.' "
5	Adam Clarke[16]	Yes	*"Upon thy belly shalt thou go* — thou shalt no longer walk erect, but mark the ground equally with thy hands and feet."

6	Leupold[17]	Yes/No — open to both — not necessarily a complete transformation but leans toward few, if any changes	"The first element is, 'upon thy belly thou shalt go.' This does not necessarily mean that a complete transformation of the serpent took place, so that "form and movements of the serpent were altered" (Keil). Some speak quite boldly at this point about a former erect posture, as though, for example, the serpent had strutted about proudly as a cock. It has been rightly pointed out that several parallels are available. Man worked before the Fall and still works since. Now work is in a measure a punishment. It seems likely that the rainbow existed before the Flood; but since that time it is a pledge of God's covenant."
7	Matthew Poole[18]	Yes	"If the serpent did so before the fall, what then was natural, is now become painful and shameful to it, as naked-ness and some other things were to man. But it seems more probable that this serpent before the fall either had feet, or rather did go with its breast erect, as the basilisk at this day doth; God peradventure so ordering it as a testimony that some other serpents did once go so. And so the sense of the curse being applied to this particular serpent, and to its kind, may be this: Whereas thou hadst a privilege above other kinds of serpents, whereby thou didst go with erected breast, and didst feed upon the fruits of trees and other plants; now thou shalt be brought down to the same mean and vile estate with them."
8	John Trapp[19]	Yes	"The serpent here is first cut shorter by the feet, and made to wriggle upon his belly."

9	Martin Luther	Yes	"From this some obvious conclusions follow: that before sin the serpent was a most beautiful little animal and most pleasing to man, as little mules, sheep and puppies today; moreover, that it walked upright."
10	Allen P. Ross[20]	Yes	He says nothing about how the Curse affected the serpent physically, though Ross indicates that the Curse did change him physically in some way.
11	C.F. Keil and F. Delitzsch[21]	Yes	"The form and movements of the serpent were altered . . . though we cannot form any accurate idea of its original appearance."
12	Flavius Josephus[22]	Yes	". . . had deprived him of the use of his feet."
13	Gordon Wenham[23]	No	"It is doubtful whether this implies that snakes once had legs to walk with like other animals." But he doesn't explain why he thinks it is doubtful.
14	John Sailhamer[24]	No	"This curse does not necessarily suggest that the snake had previously walked with feet and legs as the other land animals." But he doesn't explain why he calls the serpent a "snake" or why he concludes this about the Curse.

Most commentaries seem certain that it was referring to some form of erect creature and changes took place with the Curse. John Calvin was the only one of these who seemed to think that the serpent remained with the same form.[25] He said that the Curse was more of a statement to "put the serpent back in its place." Leupold leaves open either position but leans against a full transformation, leaving the serpent more in its original form. Wenham and Sailhamer more recently (1987 and 1990 respectively) both lean against the serpent changing forms but give no reasons why they believe this.

The problem with leaving the serpent "as is" is that it reduces the Curse to almost a meaningless status. If such a philosophy is to be held,

Figure 3. Serpent with legs and still crawling on its belly.

then the parallel comments by the Lord to the woman and the man should also be statements to just "put them back in their place." This raises theological issues. It would mean that the other effects of sin listed in Genesis 3, such as thorns and thistles, increased pain and sorrow for the woman, and mankind returning to dust, were merely statements to put human beings back in their place, not real changes. This seems highly illogical, as it would have death before sin in humans, with man already returning to dust (recall Romans 5:12).

Conclusion

The more logical answer is that the serpent originally had some form of legs or appendages, and these were either lost or reduced (consider how many reptiles crawl on their bellies and yet have legs, e.g., crocodiles). This seems to correlate with the plainest reading of the passage and the comparison of a Curse ("on your belly you shall go") as compared with cattle and other beasts of the field, which do have legs.

Thorns and thistles were brought forth due to the Curse (physical changes to vegetation); there were physical changes to the man and woman (increased sorrow in childbearing and increased pain in work that has been passed along). There is no reason to assume the serpent didn't undergo physical changes as well — he was a prime culprit. These physical changes due to the Curse help explain certain defense and attack structures (DAS) in animals and plants that currently dominate the world.

10. Shouldn't the woman (Eve) have been shocked that a serpent spoke?

Often, people say that they can't believe the serpent in Genesis 3 spoke, because they claim animals don't speak! Well, I wish I could tell that to my sister-in-law's Blue-Fronted Amazon Parrot that doesn't stop talking! Many types of parrots talk by mimicking, so it would be illogical to think that God didn't give this ability to other animals — especially in a perfect world.

Speaking human-sounding words and speaking intelligently, however, is not the same. Balaam's donkey, the only other example given of animals speaking in Scripture, was specially enabled by the power of *God* to speak intelligently to Balaam. Because there is no other place in Scripture that reveals Satan or demons can cause animals to speak, it makes more sense that the serpent could make the sounds capable of speech and Satan used this to his advantage. In essence, Satan likely used this feature that the original serpent had and caused it to say what he wanted.

Although this may *sound* farfetched, there should be caution about limiting what God did or didn't do in the perfect Garden. There is a possibility that many other animals had the ability to "speak" before the Curse. Many animals have types of sound-based or mimicry forms of communication today.

But the serpent was "clever" when it spoke. It made *sense* to the woman. "Woman" denotes Eve's original name as given in Genesis 2:23, when Adam named her. She was originally named Woman and it seems she wasn't given the name Eve until after sin. Throughout these chapters both names are used. Most of the time they are corresponding to the name prior to and after sin, but not always. The use of the names "man" and "Adam" were both used prior to sin for the first man. Sometimes one may see Adam and the woman referenced, so please note that the name woman is not used in any derogatory sense, but simply as a name. Since *Satan* was the one who influenced the serpent (Revelation 12:9, 20:2), it makes sense why the serpent could deliver a cogent message capable of deceiving her. The serpent apparently cooperated and was an instrument in the deception and so deserved a punishment, which God justly gave. This reminds me of Judas, who also received due punishment, even though Satan entered him (Luke 22:3).

Of course today, serpents don't speak, but the Curse in Genesis 3:14 probably had something to do with this. Recall the physical changes in Genesis 3. Perhaps this is the reason the particular kind of serpent that deceived the woman did not pass along the ability to speak or may have even become extinct since the Fall.[26]

The issue of the woman being *shocked* when she heard the serpent speak also has a couple of problems. First, everything in the Garden of Eden was new to the first couple — they'd only been alive for a short time. Even a bug, cat, or dinosaur would all be new, so they wouldn't have been shocked at a talking serpent.

God also programmed language into Adam and Eve (since they were able to speak immediately with God), which would have included some words that describe animals and their capabilities. So it shouldn't have been *shocking* to see or hear something for the first time if you're already "programmed" to know about something like talking animals.

11. Was Satan the actual serpent in the Garden?

This interpretation primarily comes from Revelation 12:9 and 20:2 without much regard to other passages, such as Genesis 3.

So the great dragon was cast out, that serpent of old, called the Devil and Satan, who deceives the whole world; he was cast to the earth, and his angels were cast out with him (Revelation 12:9).

He laid hold of the dragon, that serpent of old, who is the Devil and Satan, and bound him for a thousand years (Revelation 20:2).

These verses give excellent information about Satan and his many names as well as his involvement back in Eden, being the serpent of old. But does this eliminate that he used a real serpent? Not necessarily. The whole of Scripture needs to be consulted.

We read in Genesis 3 that there was a real serpent and it received a real physical curse to crawl on its belly and eat dust for the duration of its life (Genesis 3:14). Satan is not a physical being, although he can operate in the physical realm (Job 1–2). He is a spiritual being that operates in the spiritual realm as evidenced in many passages that detail his spiritual attributes, such as 1 Peter 5:8; Matthew 16:23; Acts 5:3; and Ephesians 6:12.

Behold My hands and My feet, that it is I Myself. Handle Me and see, for a spirit does not have flesh and bones as you see I have (Luke 24:39).

The Bible seems to portray Satan and his angels as disembodied spirits. So then, how can both Satan and a real serpent be the culprit? From other passages we find an important principle. Satan and demons can enter into people and animals and influence them. For example, Judas was entered by Satan in Luke 22:3; Peter was influenced by Satan[27] (Matthew 16:23); and the swine were entered by Legion, which consisted of many demons (Mark 5, Matthew 8).

Although such things may escape us, God easily sees when Satan is influencing someone and will often speak directly to Satan. Beginning in Ezekiel 28:11, for example, God is speaking to Satan who was influencing the king of Tyre. In the sections prior to this, the *Word of the Lord* was said to Tyre itself (Ezekiel 27:2), then to the ruler of Tyre (Ezekiel 28:2), and now *a lament* (expression of grief or mourning for past events) beginning in Ezekiel 28:11 to the king of Tyre. This one specifically was directed to the one influencing the king of Tyre — Satan — since the person, the king of Tyre, was never a model of perfection, nor was he on the mount of God, nor was he in the Garden of Eden, nor was he perfect in his ways from the day he was created, till iniquity was found in him (v. 15).

In Isaiah 14, the passage speaks to the king of Babylon and in some parts to Satan, who was influencing him. In Scripture, God sometimes speaks both to the person and to the one influencing that person — Satan.

So there is no stretch to understand that the Lord is speaking to the serpent and Satan in Genesis 3. Genesis 3:14 is said to the serpent and then Genesis 3:15 is said to Satan who is influencing the serpent. Martin Luther states it this way:

> Let us therefore, establish in the first place that the serpent is a real serpent, but one that has been entered and taken over by Satan.[28]

The Bible tells us that Satan used a real serpent to deceive Eve. And because of his entrance into the serpent, he can rightly be called the "serpent of old" or "great dragon" in Revelation.

12. Was Adam with Eve when she spoke to the serpent?

Here at Answers in Genesis, there are people on both sides of this friendly in-house debate. The Scriptures say:

> Now the serpent was more cunning than any beast of the field which the LORD God had made. And he said to the woman, "Has God indeed said, 'You shall not eat of every tree of the garden'?" And the woman said to the serpent, "We may eat the fruit of the trees of the garden; but of the fruit of the tree which is in the midst of the garden, God has said, 'You shall not eat it, nor shall you touch it, lest you die.' " Then the serpent said to the woman, "You will not surely die. For God knows that in the day you eat of it your eyes will be opened, and you will be like God, knowing good and evil." So when the woman saw that the tree was good for food, that it was pleasant to the eyes, and a tree desirable to make one wise, she took of its fruit and ate. She also gave to her husband with her, and he ate (Genesis 3:1–6).

Those who believe Adam was present with Eve (the woman) during the temptation point to the fact that Genesis 3:6 states that Eve gave some fruit to her husband who was "with her." At first glance, this seems to settle the matter, but arguments have been raised against this.

First, the Scripture does not necessarily state that Adam was with Eve when she was deceived. It only mentions Adam *when she ate*. Many believe the phrase "with her" is out of context when applying it to the events in the previous section.

Many believe a small amount of time passed to permit Adam to arrive on the scene to see her pick the fruit, eat it, and give some to him to eat. Part of the reason for this small amount of time is due to events that took place between Eve speaking to the serpent and Adam eating. For example,

Eve saw that the fruit was good to eat. How could she know the fruit was good to eat? Perhaps she saw an animal eat some of the fruit — maybe even the serpent. Keep in mind that man was forbidden to eat from the tree of the knowledge of good and evil, but the Bible gives no indication that the animals couldn't have eaten from it.

Second, in Genesis 3:17, God rightly charges Adam of heeding the voice of his wife. This likely indicates there was a conversation between Adam and Eve after her discussion with the serpent. This will be covered in more detail in the coming paragraphs.

Figure 4. Eve giving Adam the fruit (as depicted in the Creation Museum)

In fact, the Bible never says the serpent spoke to Adam and Eve, but only to Eve. Only Eve responded, and it is highly unlikely that Adam wouldn't respond at all if he was involved in the conversation — especially with the blatant errors spoken in the conversation. Logically, it is easier to deceive one person than two anyway. Note the clever deception by the serpent in that he did not go by the Lord God's created order. He did not go to Adam first, but instead went directly for Eve, unlike God, who first questioned Adam (Genesis 3:9).

There was probably some small amount of time between the temptation and Eve's eating the fruit, so the question arises whether or not it was enough time for Adam to arrive. Expositor Dr. John Gill wrote of Genesis 3:6:

> ... *and gave also to her husband with her*; and gave also to her
> husband with her; that he might eat as well as she, and partake of
> the same benefits and advantages she hoped to reap from hence;
> for no doubt it was of good will, and not ill will, that she gave it to
> him; and when she offered it to him, it is highly probable she
> made use of arguments with him, and pressed him hard to it, tell-
> ing him what delicious food it was, as well as how useful it would
> be to him and her. The Jews infer from hence, that Adam was with
> her all the while, and heard the discourse between the serpent
> and her, yet did not interpose nor dissuade his wife from eating
> the fruit, and being prevailed upon by the arguments used; or
> however through a strong affection for his wife, that she might
> not die alone, he did as she had done.[29]

Gill believed there was a discussion between Eve and Adam after her
deception. He even believed Eve was indeed alone when deceived:

> *And he said to the woman*; being alone, which he took the
> advantage of; not the serpent, but Satan in it; just as the angel
> spoke in Balaam's ass.[30]

John Calvin stated in his commentary:

> *And gave also unto her husband with her.* From these words,
> some conjecture that Adam was present when his wife was
> tempted and persuaded by the serpent, which is by no means
> credible. Yet it might be that he soon joined her, and that, even
> before the woman tasted the fruit of the tree, she related the con-
> versation held with the serpent, and entangled him with the same
> fallacies by which she herself had been deceived. Others refer the
> particle (*immah*) "with her," to the conjugal bond, which may be
> received. But because Moses simply relates that he ate the fruit

taken from the hands of his wife, the opinion has been commonly received, that he was rather captivated with her allurements than persuaded by Satan's impostures. For this purpose the declaration of Paul is adduced, "Adam was not deceived, but the woman" (1 Timothy 2:14). But Paul in that place, as he is teaching that the origin of evil was from the woman, only speaks comparatively. Indeed, it was not only for the sake of complying with the wishes of his wife, that he transgressed the law laid down for him; but being drawn by her into fatal ambition, he became partaker of the same defection with her. And truly Paul elsewhere states that sin came not by the woman, but by Adam himself (Romans 5:12). Then, the reproof which soon afterwards follows, "Behold, Adam is as one of us," clearly proves that he also foolishly coveted more than was lawful, and gave greater credit to the flatteries of the devil than to the sacred word of God.[31]

Poole's commentary agrees:

Gave also unto her husband with her, who by this time was returned to her, and who now was with her; or, that he might eat with her, and take his part of that fruit.[32]

So these men didn't see that Adam needed to be with Eve when she was deceived. Even Trapp's commentary leaves open the possibility that Adam wasn't with Eve the whole time:

And gave it also to her husband. It is probable, saith the same author, that Adam stood by all the time of the disputation; therefore his sin was the greater, that he rebuked not the serpent, &c. And again, I cannot believe, said he, but that the devils in the serpent did as well tempt Adam as Eve, though first they began with her, as a further means of enticing him. Others are of another mind, as that the tempter set upon the woman alone and apart from her husband, as she was curiously prying into the pleasures of the garden; that the serpent crept into Paradise unseen of Adam, who was to keep beasts out of it; that he remained there without being seen by him, and crept out again when he had done his feat; that when she gave him the fruit, she gave him also a relation of the serpent's promise concerning the force of that fruit, that it would make them wise as God, knowing good and evil, &c., whence he is said to have hearkened to her voice. {Genesis 3:17} And surely, every Adam hath still his Eve, every David his Bathsheba, a tempter in his own bosom, his own flesh, whereby he is so soon "drawn away, and enticed" as a fish by the bait — beauty is a hook without a bait, as one saith — till "when lust hath conceived," as here it did in Eve, "it bringeth forth sin; and sin, when it is finished, bringeth forth death." {James 1:14–15} Satan hath only a persuasive sleight, not an enforcing might. It is our own concupiscence that carrieth the greatest stroke.[33]

In *The Genesis Record*, Henry Morris says:

As the prototype of all sinners, Eve felt impelled to lead Adam to participate in the same sin. She therefore plucked more of the fruit and brought it to her husband, urging him to eat it as well. No doubt, she used the same arguments the serpent had used, also adding the personal testimony that she had eaten the delicious fruit herself without harmful effect.

Adam, however, "was not deceived" (1 Timothy 3:14). Whether this statement by the Apostle Paul means that Adam was fully aware that he was willfully defying God, or whether it simply means that Adam was not the initial one whom Satan attacked with this deception, may not be completely clear.[34]

Paul says in 1 Timothy:

For Adam was formed first, then Eve. And Adam was not deceived, but the woman being deceived, fell into transgression (1 Timothy 2:13–14).

The passage says Eve, and not Adam, was deceived, but this still doesn't shed light on whether Adam was with Eve or if he showed up afterward. In both cases (Adam with Eve or Adam not with Eve), 1 Timothy 2:13–14 could easily apply. If Adam was not with Eve, then obviously he wouldn't have been deceived. He could have eaten knowing he was sinning, regardless of knowing the serpent had deceived Eve.

Then to Adam He said, "Because you have heeded the voice of your wife, and have eaten from the tree of which I commanded you, saying, 'You shall not eat of it': Cursed is the ground for your sake; in toil you shall eat of it all the days of your life" (Genesis 3:17).

There is no indication that Adam listened to the voice of the serpent, but he *did* listen to the voice of his wife. Since God said that Adam *listened* to the voice of his wife, then two scenarios could apply:

1. Scenario 1: This was her voice when she responded to the serpent.
2. Scenario 2: This was a conversation after she spoke with the serpent.

Analyzing Scenario 1

If Adam listened to the voice of his wife when she responded to the serpent, then why didn't he correct her when she misquoted God's command?[35] She said:

From the fruit of the trees of the garden we may eat; but from the fruit of the tree which is in the middle of the garden, God has said, "You shall not eat from it **or touch it**, or you will die" (Genesis

3:2–3; NASB, emphasis added).

Eve left out some key words and then added to God's Word:

> From **any** tree of the garden you may eat **freely**; but from the tree of the knowledge of good and evil you shall not eat, for in the day that you eat from it you will **surely** die (Genesis 2:16–17; NASB, emphasis added).

She removed "any" and "freely" but added "or touch it" and even misstated "surely die" as merely "die" (another thing she did was demote Lord God to merely God, which is how the serpent addressed God in a demeaning manner). If Adam listened to his wife's erroneous words here, then he could have been deceived into believing something other than what God said. However, 1 Timothy indicates Adam was not deceived, so this is likely not the case.

Also, since he was not deceived, Adam should have corrected his wife's mistaken response, especially since he knew what was right (James 4:17). If this were the case, he would have been sinning before he ate, yet the Lord didn't mention it or give a rebuke for these potentially failed actions.[36]

But take note that if Adam had only listened to what Eve said to the serpent (Genesis 3:2–3), and *heeded* it, then he would not have even touched the fruit, let alone eat it!

Analyzing Scenario 2

Eve conversed with Adam and he ate (but not by deception), thus with this scenario they *had* to have a conversation soon *after* the woman conversed with the serpent, which is what Gill, Calvin, Trapp, Morris, and others have pointed out.

God said nothing of Adam listening to the voice of the serpent, but only that he listened to Eve. In fact, Adam only blamed his wife, not the serpent, which may indicate that he wasn't aware of the serpent's discussion with her.

Though this conversation between Adam and his wife is not mentioned in the early portions of the text in Genesis 3, it does give further support that the time reference in verse 6 indicates that time *had passed* from Eve's conversation with the serpent and her taking a bite and giving some to her husband. Apparently there were events that were not entirely recorded in detail, such as this conversation.

This time reference and new conversation between Eve and Adam is further support that the phrase "with her" in Genesis 3:6 would be out of context with the prior events — when she was being deceived by the serpent. So Scenario 2 seems *much more* plausible, though one should not be dogmatic.

Regardless, this surely didn't take long from the serpent's deception to when Eve desired the fruit and spoke to her husband and then ate.[37] We should refrain from being dogmatic that Adam was there the whole time because so little is given in Scripture.

Without question though, Adam was with his wife when she ate, so he had no excuse for not knowing what he ate. He knew it was fruit from the tree of the knowledge of good and evil and knowingly sinned when he ate.

13. Who sinned first – Adam or Satan?

When Christians speak of Adam being the first sinner, this refers to Paul saying:

> Therefore, just as through one man sin entered the world, and death through sin, and thus death spread to all men, because all sinned (Romans 5:12).

It means that sin *entered* the world through Adam — that is, Adam is the one credited with sin's entrance and hence the subsequent entrance of death and suffering and the need for a Savior and a last Adam (1 Corinthians 15:45). When we look back at Genesis 3, it is true that Satan had rebelled and also the woman (later named Eve) sinned prior to Adam.

The sin of the woman (Eve)

There were several things that Eve did wrong prior to eating the fruit. The first was her misspeaking while responding to the serpent. When the serpent (who was speaking the words of Satan) asked in Genesis 3:1, "Has God indeed said, 'You shall not eat of every tree of the garden?' " her response was less than perfect:

> And the woman said to the serpent, "We may eat the fruit of the trees of the garden; but of the fruit of the tree which is in the midst of the garden, God has said, 'You shall not eat it, *nor shall you touch it*, lest you die' " (Genesis 3:2–3; emphasis added).

Compare this to what God had commanded in Genesis 2:16–17:

> And the LORD God commanded the man, saying, "Of every tree of the garden you may freely eat; but of the tree of the knowledge of good and evil you shall not eat, for in the day that you eat of it you shall surely die."

The woman made four mistakes in her response:

1. She added the command not to *touch* the fruit ("nor shall you touch it"). This may even be in contradiction with the command to tend the Garden (Genesis 2:15), which may have necessitated touching the tree and the fruit from time to time. This also makes the command from God seem exceptionally harsh.

2. She amended that God allowed them to *freely* eat. This makes God out to be less gracious.

3. She amended that God allowed them to freely eat from *every* tree. Again, this makes God out to be less gracious.

4. She amended the meaning of die. The Hebrew in Genesis 2:17 is "die-die" (*muwth-muwth*), which is often translated as "surely die" or literally as "dying you shall die," which indicates the beginning of dying, an ingressive sense. In other words, if they would have eaten the fruit, then Adam and Eve would have *begun to die* and would return to dust (which is what happened when they ate in Genesis 3:19). If they were meant to die right then, Genesis 2:17 should have used *muwth* only once, as is used in the Hebrew meaning "dead," "died," or "die" in an absolute sense, and not *beginning to* die or *surely* die as die-die is commonly used. What Eve said was "die" (*muwth*) once instead of the way God said it in Genesis 2:17 as "die-die" (*muwth-muwth*). So she changed God's Word to appear harsher again by saying they would die almost immediately. (See also Genesis 2:17: "you shall surely die.")

Often we are led to believe that Satan merely deceived Eve with the statement that "You will not surely die?" in Genesis 3:4. But we neglect the cleverness/cunningness that God indicates that the serpent had in Genesis 3:1. Note also that the exchange seems to suggest that Eve may have been willingly led: that is, she had already changed what God had said.

If you take a closer look, the serpent argued against Eve with an extremely clever ploy. He went back and argued against her incorrect words, using the correct phraseology that God used in Genesis 2:17 ("die-die" (*muwth-muwth*). This, in a deceptive way, used the proper sense of die that God stated in Genesis 2:17 against Eve's mistaken view. Imagine the conversation in simplified terms like this:

> **God says**: Don't eat or you will begin to die.
> **Eve says**: We can't eat or we will die *immediately*.
> **Serpent says**: You will not *begin* to die.

This was very clever of Satan. This is not an isolated incident either. When Satan tried tempting Jesus (Matthew 4), Jesus said "it is written" and quoted Scripture (Matthew 4:4). The second time Satan tried quoting Scripture (i.e., God) but did it deceptively just as he had done to Eve (Matthew 4:5–6). Of course, Jesus was not deceived, but corrected Satan's twisted use of Scripture (Matthew 4:7). But because of Eve's mistaken view of God's Word, it was easier for her to be deceived by Satan's misuse of Scripture.

From there, she started down the slope into sin by being enticed by the fruit (James 1:14–15). This culminated with eating the forbidden fruit and giving some to her husband and encouraging him to eat. Eve sinned against God by eating the fruit from the tree of the knowledge of good and evil prior to Adam. However, with a closer look at the text, their eyes were not opened until after Adam ate — likely only moments later (Genesis 3:7). Since Adam was created first (Eve coming from him, but both being created in God's image) and had been given the command directly, it required his sin to bring about the Fall of mankind. When Adam ate and sinned, they knew something was wrong and felt ashamed (Genesis 3:7). Sin and death had entered into the creation.

The Sin of Satan

Like Eve, Satan has sinned prior to this. His sin was pride in his beauty (Ezekiel 28:15–17) while in a perfect heaven (Isaiah 14:12), and he was cast out when imperfection was found in him (Isaiah 14:12; Revelation 12:9; Ezekiel 28:15). Then we find him in Garden of Eden (Ezekiel 28:13; Genesis 3).

Unlike Adam, Satan was not created in the image of God and was never given dominion over the world (Genesis 1:28). So his sin did not affect the creation, but merely his own person. This is likely why Satan went immediately for those who were given dominion. Being an enemy of God (and, thus, those who bear His image), he apparently wanted to do the most damage, so it was likely that his deception happened quickly.

The Responsibility of Adam

Adam failed at his responsibilities in two ways. He should have stopped his wife from eating, since he was there to observe exactly what she said and was about to eat (Genesis 3:6). Instead of listening to (and not correcting) the words of his wife (Genesis 3:17), he ate while not being deceived (1 Timothy 2:14).

Adam also arguably failed to keep/guard the garden as he was commanded in *Genesis 2:15*. God, knowing Satan would fall, gave this command to Adam, but Adam did not complete the task. But God even knew that Adam would fall short and had a plan specially prepared.

I've had some people ask me, "Why do we have to die for something Adam did?" The answer is simple — we are without excuse since we sin too (Romans 3:23, 5:12). But then some have asked, "Why did we have to inherit sin nature from Adam, which is why we sin?" We read in Hebrews:

> Even Levi, who receives tithes, paid tithes through Abraham, so to speak, for he was still in the loins of his father when Melchizedek met him (Hebrews 7:9–10).

If we follow this logic, then all of us were ultimately in Adam when he sinned. So, although we often blame Adam, the life we have was in Adam when he sinned, and the sin nature we received was because we were in

Adam when he sinned. We share in the blame and the sin as well as the punishment.

But look back further. The life that we (including Eve) have came through Adam and ultimately came from God (Genesis 2:17). God owns us and gives us our very being (Hebrews 1:3), and it is He whom we should follow instead of our own sinful inclinations. Since this first sin, we have had the need for a Savior, Jesus Christ, the Son of God who would step into history to become a man and take the punishment for humanity's sin. Such a loving feat shows that God truly loves mankind and wants to see us return to Him. God — being the Author of life, the Sustainer of life, and Redeemer of life — is truly the One we owe all things.

14. Why do we get punished for something Adam did?

When Adam sinned, his punishment was death (Genesis 2:17). Because of Adam's sin, death came upon all men. Some have said that it is harsh for God to punish all of Adam's descendants for something Adam did. But is it? Since we sin too, we all deserve death before a perfect Holy God. To assume Adam's descendants are innocent is a false assumption. Due to the sin nature received from Adam, death is coming for all since all have sinned (Romans 3:23).

It is illogical to think that two imperfect people could produce perfect offspring. Since Adam and Eve had both sinned and fell, it would be impossible for their children to be perfectly free from sin. So the real question is: why would God permit *sin nature* to pass along to Adam's descendants?[38] Doesn't that seem harsh?

Consider that the Book of Hebrews points out that Levi was in the loins (body) of his ancestor Abraham when he paid tithes to Melchizedek (Genesis 14:18–20).

If this applies to each person being "in" their ancestors, then we could say Abraham was in the body of Noah before the Flood. And Noah was in the body of his ancestor Adam when he sinned! In a sense, we were all in Adam when he sinned! This explains why we inherit a sin nature. When Adam sinned, a sin nature came over them and since we were in them and our life came from them, we inherit this nature as well.

So far, this all sounds like bad news — and it is — but there is good news:

> For since by man came death, by Man also came the resurrection of the dead. For as in Adam all die, even so in Christ all shall be made alive (1 Corinthians 15:21–22).

Through Adam, death came into the world. Jesus came and demonstrated He has power over death. Thus, those who are in Christ will be saved and death will have no sting.

> "O Death, where is your sting? O Hades, where is your victory?" The sting of death is sin, and the strength of sin is the law. But thanks be to God, who gives us the victory through our Lord Jesus Christ (1 Corinthians 15:55–57).

Although death seems to be inevitable for all, one day God will put an end to this enemy (1 Corinthians 15:26). The life that we have came through Adam and ultimately from God (Genesis 2:7). God owns us and gives us our very being (Hebrews 1:3; Acts 17:28; Colossians 1:16–18), and it is He whom we should follow instead of sin. Because of the sin of our first parents, the human race needs a Savior. Jesus Christ, the Son of God, stepped into history to take this punishment for sin. Such a loving feat shows that God loves mankind and wants to see us return to Him. God, the Author, Sustainer, and Redeemer of life, is truly the One to be praised.

15. Is original sin (sin nature) passed through the father's genetic line?

This question and variants like it have arisen in the past. Follow this reasoning:

Basis: Jesus was sinless (Hebrews 4:15; 1 John 3:5). Jesus was a descendant of Adam as per Luke 3 (in His humanity). Descendants of Adam receive original sin because they were in Adam when Adam sinned (Romans 5:12). So how did Jesus avoid having original sin?

There are several popular responses to this (basic arguments given below) that show there is no contradiction within Scripture:

1. *Father's line*: Jesus inherited genetic material from Mary (to be fully human, i.e., descendant of Adam to become *the Last Adam*) but not from Joseph, therefore, original sin must pass through the father to the offspring. This allows Jesus to avoid original sin.
2. *Sin nature is not sin*: the terms "sin nature" or "original sin" are not found in the Bible and are terms derived by humans when looking at certain passages. Sin nature is a tendency toward sin, not sin in and of itself. This avoids Jesus being a sinner.
3. *Sin nature passes spiritually*: original sin is nonmaterial and doesn't need to pass along to offspring via genetics. It is passed along spiritually by virtue that all are descendants of Adam. But God withheld original sin from entering Christ in the womb.

"Father's line" model

The first view is the *Father's line model*. Initially this sounds like a reasonable model but there are some problems associated with it.

There are no Scriptures that connect the virgin birth to sin or sin nature. The reason for the virgin birth is a miraculous entrance into the world by fulfilling prophecies such as Genesis 3:15 and Isaiah 7:14. Caution should be exercised when adding other implications to the virgin birth.

Second, if sin nature is materialistic and passed through the father while reproduction occurs, then, in theory, a "clone" (of sorts anyway) using two sets of female DNA (resulting in only a female) could be sinless and Jesus would no longer be unique as being separate from sinners (Hebrews 7:26).

The punishment for sin is death (Genesis 2:17, 3:19; Romans 5:12) and theoretically if one of these "clones" was without sin nature and didn't sin, then they could not die and should live eternally, hence, a means of eternal life without the need for Jesus Christ (John 14:6). Jesus, who was sinless, still died on the Cross without being a sinner; but in order to die, He *became* sin for us (Hebrews 9:28; 2 Corinthians 5:21).

Often in today's culture people try to find materialistic explanations due to influences of materialism and naturalism (foundations of evolution) that exclude supernaturalism and the spiritual realm. But truth, logic, information, souls, mind, sin nature, and so on are not material entities.

It is vital to realize the difference between the material and the immaterial in this discussion. Consider the following:

1. Adam

Adam originally had perfect DNA[39] (Genesis 1:31, Deuteronomy 32:4), and yet there was no original sin found in him at the start. Sin nature came about when Adam *sinned*. Were genetic changes involved in Genesis 3? Perhaps, but such a position should not be held dogmatically. But the fact that genes can exist *without* sin nature, shows that sin nature is not intrinsically bound to genetics.

2. Life is passed along and it is non-material

Life also passed from Adam to all of us. But originally Adam's life came from God when God breathed life into him (Genesis 2:7), even though his entire body was formed with DNA, flesh, bones, etc. This immaterial life from God was independent of Adam's body, since it was "breathed" into it.

3. Satan/Demons

Satan and demons may be the pinnacle to show that sin nature is not bound to material means. Satan is spirit and he can tempt, influence, and even enter into people (Luke 22:3 with Judas) or animals (Genesis 3 with the serpent, and in Mark 5:1–17 with Legion and the swine). They have sinned and continue to sin (having their own sin nature) *without human genes*. This shows that sin nature is not confined to human DNA.

"Sin nature is not sin" model

Instead of avoiding sin nature, this model teaches that sin nature is not sin in and of itself but the tendency toward sin, and Jesus, even with this tendency, did not sin. In part, this model derives from Hebrews 4:15, meaning that Jesus had to have a sin nature in order to be tempted just as we are. In other words, the model teaches that one can be justified in sinning because "man couldn't help it" and therefore cannot rightly be compared to Jesus who wouldn't have undergone what the rest of us underwent. This model also assumes the peccability of Christ, which is hotly debated.[40]

For we do not have a High Priest who cannot sympathize with our weaknesses, but was in all points tempted as we are, yet without sin (Hebrews 4:15).

Obviously, Jesus was tempted *externally*, having fasted 40 days and nights, and then Satan himself tempted him three times (Matthew 4).

Jesus was tempted *internally* as well if one looks at the Garden of Gethsemane (Matthew 26:39, 42, 44). Jesus in His humanity was "tempted" to give up the cup that had been passed to Him, but still remained within the will of God, not His human will. Another case that reveals Christ's internal temptations is Hebrews 2:18, which says:

> For in that He Himself has suffered, being tempted, He is able to aid those who are tempted.

Christ was suffering due to temptation. Also take note of Paul's comment:

> No temptation has overtaken you except such as is common to man; but God is faithful, who will not allow you to be tempted beyond what you are able, but with the temptation will also make the way of escape, that you may be able to bear it (1 Corinthians 10:13).

God doesn't permit one to be tempted more than one can bear. Christ — our perfect example and God incarnate — was tempted to an extreme that we have not had to bear. A temptation, in and of itself, is not sin. Temptation may lead to sin, and here is the progression described in James:

> But each one is tempted when he is drawn away by his own desires and enticed. Then, when desire has conceived, it gives birth to sin; and sin, when it is full-grown, brings forth death (James 1:14–15).

Note in the progression that being drawn away by our own human desires and enticed is also *not sin*. When desires *conceive* or are put into action or even thought (Matthew 5:28), then it becomes sin. When we look at Genesis 3, we find this progression with the woman, Eve:

1. Tempted by the serpent
2. Drawn away and enticed by desiring the fruit
3. Desire conceived when she ate, *thus her action of sin.*

Of course, Adam was the representative for humankind, and when he ate, all humanity became doomed to the Curse. Turning to Matthew 4 in the Garden of Gethsemane, Jesus was perhaps enticed by the desire of not fulfilling what He was there to do. And yet, this desire *did not conceive* and Jesus did not sin.

Does this mean Jesus had original sin then? This second view points out that "original sin" and "sin nature" are phrases that are not found in Scripture, but are derived from Genesis 3 and summed up in Romans 5 (verse 12 specifically), elaborated on in Romans 7:13–25, and, by common definition, means *the tendency toward sin as a consequence for descendants of Adam because of his sin.* But in the same respect, all have become sinners as a result (Romans 3:23, 5:19).

Original sin means having an indirect part in Adam's sin and thus tending toward sin. In this model, Adam was the responsible party and died for his sin. We are not responsible for that sin but for the sins we commit ourselves. John 8:24 gives an indication that people die for their *own* sins, not necessarily the sin nature that was inherent from Adam. This sin nature then is not sin itself, but explains why mankind sins and tends toward it.

Having a part of Christ being directly given to Mary from God — the Holy Spirit — shows that Christ is both fully God and fully human (Colossians 1:16, 2:9; John 1:1–3; Hebrews 2:14). In one sense, it excused Jesus for not being in Adam when he sinned but since His life also came through Mary, it goes back to Adam as well.

The model also teaches that since Christ has direct lineage to Adam through Mary, this shows that He inherits this nature in His humanity, and since He was without sin, then sin nature *cannot* be sin but merely the tendency toward sin or in other words, to overtly make desires conceive into sin. The judgment of Revelation 20:11–15 also supports this notion since the people there are judged "according to their works" (verses 12 and 13) as opposed to being judged for their nature. So from the moment of fertilization, people's desires conceive into sin. Yet Christ's desires never turned to sin.

Scripture never records if Satan ever *tried* to tempt God the Father, but it would seem unlikely since He cannot be tempted (James 1:13), but he did tempt Jesus. In Christ's humanity, Satan had an opportunity to tempt Christ; yet Christ did not succumb.

Christians, although having sin nature, do not *continually* sin (1 John 3:9). Therefore, they can resist sin, even though sin nature has reign over them. Consider Adam and Christ. Adam sinned without sin nature, and yet Jesus did not sin, having such a nature in this model.

One problematic issue in this model comes down to the interpretation of original sin. If one was in Adam when Adam sinned, then he is a sinner because Adam sinned. So although this model downplays that mankind was involved in Adam's sin, it doesn't completely remove it.

Another objection relates to an internal temptation of Christ. Never once did Satan enter into Christ, for he cannot. So any alleged internal temptation of Christ must come from Himself. A desire to rebel against God is needed to conceive into sin and Christ has no such desire in Himself. Recall, that James 1:13 says that God cannot be tempted, and Jesus being the Creator God (John 1; Colossians 1; and Hebrews 1) cannot be tempted internally, i.e., He cannot desire to rebel against God, i.e., Himself. This is different from someone trying to tempt Him. Christ's own desires would not lead Him toward rebellion against God. This makes sense because there are both *righteous* desires and *evil* desires.

So why was Jesus in anguish in the Garden of Gethsemane? In addition to the anguish of the terrible experience He was about to face, it was morally wrong for Him to be crucified. One possible reason Christ felt torn was because it was wrong to punish the sinless with death (i.e.,

Himself), yet it had to be done for love and salvation of mankind as an atoning sacrifice. Any desires of Christ in the Garden of Gethsemane could not have been anything but a *righteous* desire (Hebrews 12:2) — death should not be the punishment for the Son of God, but had to be done for grace. Christ was not tempted internally to sin but the desire to do two different "right" things. So this second model fails on several counts.

"Sin nature passes spiritually" model

Unlike the first model, this third model does not limit sin nature to a physical entity that needs to be passed down. Hence there is no problem for sin natures in Satan and demons. This model assumes that original sin is sin, unlike the previous model.

This model takes the position that original sin *is not required* for one to be tempted in every way. It goes back to the woman in the Garden of Eden and points out the temptations prior to original sin. When we look at Adam and the woman, we find that a person can exist without sin nature and still be tempted both externally and internally (the woman desiring the fruit and taking it), but then sinning by following through when she and Adam ate.

Therefore, when Christ was conceived by the Holy Spirit, there was no intrinsic original sin passed to Christ, while still using Mary's genetic material[41] to become a descendant of Adam. Such a task would be no problem for the Creator of the universe.

To summarize, this view holds that sin nature is not physical and, thus, not passed along by genetic means but by spiritual means.

Consider that "in Adam all die, even so in Christ all shall be made alive" (1 Corinthians 15:22).

1. Original sin translated to death for all.
2. Salvation from death translated to being made alive.

Salvation and eternal life in Christ is the direct opposite of original sin and death in Adam. Salvation is passed to people spiritually, not by physical means, and definitely not by genetic means. On this model, there is no reason to assume then that original sin was anything less than passed down by spiritual means; however, Romans 7:13–25 seems to locate the sinful tendencies as being part of the flesh (Greek *sarx*, meaning flesh or body). He states that nothing good dwells in his flesh (v. 18), that there was a law in his body warring against his mind (v. 23), and seeks deliverance from his [physical] body of death (v. 24).

It seems particularly difficult to explain this last view in completely laymen terms, because it is not based on any physical mechanism like the previous two. So let me say this: by virtue that we are sinners due to being descendants of Adam, we automatically receive sin nature not by any physical means, but spiritual means, and Christ, being God, simply doesn't receive it by virtue that He is the Son of God.

Conclusion: Mysteries belong to God

The secret things belong to the LORD our God, but those things which are revealed belong to us and to our children forever, that we may do all the words of this law (Deuteronomy 29:29).

In a discussion like this, it is good to keep in mind that there are many mysteries and secrets that belong to God. Even these explanations merely touch the surface and require years of research and books to cover this difficult topic. But the hope is that this short overview gives some food for thought.

But one lesson can be easily learned here: be wary of appealing solely to materialistic explanations in a world that is both spiritual and material.

16. Biblically, could death have existed before sin?

Death and sin — these are two things today's society seems to want to avoid in a conversation! In today's secular society, kids have been taught for generations that death goes back for millions of years. But there is a huge contrast when you open the pages of Scripture beginning in Genesis.

The Bible is the authority on the past (as well as the authority on scientific and theological aspects), and it is logical that the Bible should be the authority on the issue of death and its relationship with sin. Getting a big picture of sin and death and how they are related in the Bible can make us better witnesses to today's culture.

Everything Was Originally Perfect

God saw everything that he had made, and indeed it was very good. So the evening and the morning were the sixth day (Genesis 1:31).

He is the Rock, His work is perfect; for all His ways are justice, A God of truth and without injustice; righteous and upright is He (Deuteronomy 32:4).

When God finished creating at the end of day 6, He declared everything "very good" — it was

Figure 5. A very good creation

perfect. God's work of creation is perfect. We expect nothing less of a perfect God.

What was this "perfect" or "very good" creation like? Were animals dying? Was man dying? Let's look closer at what the Bible teaches.

Originally Vegetarian

> And God said, "See, I have given you every herb that yields seed which is on the face of all the earth, and every tree whose fruit yields seed; to you it shall be for food. Also, to every beast of the earth, to every bird of the air, and to everything that creeps on the earth, in which there is life, I have given every green herb for food"; and it was so (Genesis 1:29–30).

We know that animals and man were not eating meat originally according to Genesis 1:29–30. So meat-eaters today were all vegetarian *originally*, which also points to death not being part of the original creation. Plants are not "alive" in the biblical sense of *nephesh chayyah*, only animals and man. So plants being eaten did not mean death existed before the Fall.[42] One would not expect a God of life to be a *god of death*. When we look at God's restoration in Revelation 21–22, there will be no death, pain, or suffering.

If a Christian wants to side with the atheistic view of a world where death existed for millions of years using the majority of the fossil layers as their evidence of slow gradual accumulation instead of a global Flood, then they have major problems.[43] The fossil layers consist of many animals that have the remains of other animals in their stomach contents.[44] As we'll discuss later, Scripture tells us that sin brought about animal death, something that did not occur prior to the Fall. This rules out many of the rock layers as being evidence of million of years because the Lord declared that everything was originally vegetarian. The Flood of Noah's day is a much better explanation of the rock layers, which show animals eating other animals after sin.

Death Is a Punishment

And the LORD God commanded the man, saying, "Of every tree of the garden you may freely eat; but of the tree of the knowledge of good and evil you shall not eat, for in the day that you eat of it you shall surely die" (Genesis 2:16–17).

God gave the command in Genesis 2:16–17 that sin would be punishable by death. This is significant when we look at the big picture of death. If death in *any* form was around prior to God's declaration in Genesis 1:31 that everything was "very good," then death would be very good too — hence not a punishment at all.

Some have pointed out that this passage is not referring to animal death. In one sense, we agree with them: this verse was not directed toward animals. But by the same logic, this command was only directed toward Adam, yet Eve died and so do we (Adam's descendants) for sin. This shows the all-encompassing impact of the sin-death relationship.

Adam Knew What "Die" Meant

Some people have brought up the objection that if there was no death existing in the world, then how did Adam know what God meant in Genesis 2:17.

God, the author of language, programmed Adam with language when He created him, as they conversed right from the start on day 6 (see Genesis 2). Since God makes things perfectly, Adam knew what death meant — even if he did not have experiential knowledge of it. In fact, he probably understood it better than any of us because he had a perfect mind, uncorrupted by sin and the Curse.

Sin Brought Animal Death

The first recorded death and passages referring to death as a reality came with sin in Genesis 3 when the serpent, Eve, and Adam all were disobedient to God. Please note that what happened is the first *hint* that things will die:

So the LORD God said to the serpent, "Because you have done this, you are cursed more than all cattle, and more than every beast of the field; on your belly you shall go, and you shall eat dust *all the days of your life* (Genesis 3:14, emphasis added).

Genesis 3:14 indicates that animals, which were cursed along with the serpent, would no longer live forever but have a limited life (*all the days of your life*). This is the first hint of animal death. Since animals were cursed, they too would now die.

Though this particular verse doesn't rule out animal death prior to sin, its placement with sin and the Curse in Genesis 3 may very well be significant. The first recorded death of animals comes in Genesis 3:21, when God covered Adam and Eve with coats of *skins* to replace the fig leaf coverings they had assumed would cover their nakedness.

Also for Adam and his wife the LORD God made tunics of skin, and clothed them (Genesis 3:21).

Figure 6. The Lord's sacrifice to make coats of skins for Adam and Eve

Abel apparently mimicked something like this when he sacrificed from his flocks (fat portions) in Genesis 4:4, as did Noah after the Flood in Genesis 8:20. The Israelites did this as well, giving sin offerings of lambs, doves, etc.

Figure 7. Noah offering sacrifices

The punishment for sin was death, so something had to die. Rightly, Adam and Eve deserved to die, but we serve a God of grace, mercy, and love. And out of His love and His mercy, He basically gave us a "grace period" to repent.

The Lord sacrificed an animal to cover this sin. It was not enough to *take away* sin, but merely offered a temporary covering. This shows how much more valuable mankind is than animals (see also Matthew 6:26, 12:12). The punishment for sinning against an infinitely holy God is an infinite punishment, and animals are not infinite. They simply cannot take that punishment. We needed a perfect and infinite sacrifice that could take the infinite punishment from an infinite God. Jesus Christ, the Son of God, who is infinite, could take that punishment. These animal sacrifices foreshadowed Jesus Christ who was the ultimate, perfect, infinite sacrifice for our sins on the Cross. Hebrews reveals:

> And according to the law almost all things are purified with blood, and without shedding of blood there is no remission (Hebrews 9:22).

This is why Jesus had to die, and this is why animals were sacrificed to cover sin. These passages make it clear that animal death has a relationship with *human* sin as well as the fact that it came *after* sin.

Sin Brought Human Death

This same type of proclamation that animals will ultimately die (*all the days of your life*) comes back in Genesis 3:17, where man would also die (*all the days of your life*). Like the animals, man would die in fulfillment of what was said in Genesis 2:17.

> To Adam He said, "Because you have heeded the voice of your wife, and have eaten from the tree of which I commanded you, saying, 'You shall not eat of it': Cursed is the ground for your sake; in toil you shall eat of it *all the days of your life*" (Genesis 3:17, emphasis added).

Some have stated that they believe this was only a spiritual death, but God made it clear in Genesis 3:19 by adding that humanity will return to the dust from which we came, which makes it clear it was not excluding a physical death.

> In the sweat of your face you shall eat bread till you return to the ground, for out of it you were taken; for dust you are, and to dust you shall return" (Genesis 3:19).

Even Paul, when speaking of human death, specifically says:

> Therefore, just as through one man sin entered into the world, and death through sin, and thus death spread to all men, because all sinned (Romans 5:12).

> The last enemy that will be destroyed is death (1 Corinthians 15:26).

> Nevertheless death reigned from Adam to Moses, even over those who had not sinned according to the likeness of the transgression of Adam, who is a type of Him who was to come (Romans 5:14).

For if by the one man's offense death reigned through the one, much more those who receive abundance of grace and of the gift of righteousness will reign in life through the One, Jesus Christ (Romans 5:17).

If the death God mentioned is only spiritual, then why did Jesus have to die physically — or rise physically? If the Curse meant only spiritual death, then the gospel is undermined.

It is true that Adam and Eve didn't die the *exact* day they ate, as some seem to think Genesis 2:17 implies. The Hebrew is die-die (*muwth-muwth*), which is often translated as "surely die" or literally as "dying you shall die," which indicates the beginning of dying (i.e., an ingressive sense). At that point, Adam and Eve began to die and would return to dust. If they were meant to have died right then, the text should have used *muwth* only once, as is used in the Hebrew meaning "dead, died, or die" and not "*beginning to* die" or "*surely* die."

Does the Bible Teach Death before Sin?

The Bible tells us very clearly that there was no death before sin from many passages. In fact, there are *no Bible verses* indicating there was death prior to sin.

The only reason some people try to insert death before sin is to fit man's ideas of "millions of years" of death from a uniformitarian view of the fossil record into the Bible. But this makes a mockery of God's statement that everything was very good in Genesis 1:31. Death, animals eating other animals, thorns, cancer, tumors, and so on are not very good, and yet these are found in those fossil layers.

This leads to compromising what God plainly says to accommodate fallible man's ideas. Besides, the Scriptures reveal a global Flood in Genesis 6–8, *after sin*, which explains the vast majority of fossil layers. So one need not appeal to billions of years to explain these layers. It is better to trust what God says:

Figure 8. Death before sin is a problem for a perfect creation at the end of day 6.

> It is better to trust in the LORD, than to put confidence in man (Psalm 118:8).

Keep in mind that having death before sin also undermines the very gospel, where Jesus Christ stepped into history to conquer sin and death. In doing so, He graciously offered the free gift of salvation to all who receive him.

Conclusion

Keep in mind there are primarily two views of history (secular and Christian) with two different authorities (man's fallible reason *apart* from God and a perfect God) with conflicting views about the past.

According to the Bible, a perfect God created a perfect creation, and because of man's sin, death and suffering came into the world. But through

Figure 9. Biblical view of death

Figure 10. Mixing a secular view of death into Genesis 1

Christ we look forward to a time when there will be no more pain or death or suffering (Revelation 21:4).

In a secular worldview, there has always been death. So when *Christians* try to incorporate secular history of millions of years into their theology, two main questions arise. Was there really a change when Adam and Eve sinned? And what will heaven really be like then?

17. Why didn't Adam and Eve die the instant they ate the fruit?

The basis for this question stems from Genesis 2:17.

... but of the tree of the knowledge of good and evil you shall not eat, for in the day that you eat of it you shall surely die.

Some have claimed that the Bible doesn't necessarily mean what it says in Genesis 2:17, since Adam and Eve didn't die the moment they ate. They argue that the passage *really* means "die," not "surely die," which is what gives the implication that Adam and Eve will die on the same day they eat.

Die That Day — or Begin to Die?

It is true that Adam and Eve didn't die the exact day they ate (Genesis 5:4–5) as some seem to think Genesis 2:17 implies. So either God was in error or man's interpretation is in error. Since God *cannot* lie (Hebrews 6:18), then fallible humans must be making the mistake.

Let's take a look at where the confusion arises. The Hebrew phrase in English is more literally:

"Tree knowledge good evil eat day eat die (dying) die"

The Hebrew is, literally, *die-die* (*muwth-muwth*) with two different verb tenses (dying and die), which can be translated as "surely die" or "dying you shall die." This indicates the beginning of dying, an ingressive sense, which finally culminates with death.

At that point, Adam and Eve began to die and would return to dust (Genesis 3:19). If they were meant to die right then, the text should have simply used *muwth* only once, which means "dead, died, or die" and not *beginning to* die or *surely* die (as *muwth-muwth* is used in Hebrew). Old Testament authors understood this and used it in such a fashion, but we must remember that English translations can miss some of the nuance.

There are primarily two ways people translate: one is literal or word for word (formal equivalence) and the other is dynamic equivalence or thought-for-thought. If this is translated word for word, it would be "dying die" or "die die," which is difficult for English readers to understand, as there is no changed emphasis when a word is repeated. The Latin Vulgate by Jerome, which permits such grammatical constructions, does translate this as "dying die" or "dying you will die" (*morte morieris*). So most translations rightly use more dynamic equivalence and say "surely die."

What Is *Yom* Referring To?

With regards to the Hebrew word *yom* for day in Genesis 2:17, it refers specifically to the action of eating and not "dying die." Solomon used an almost identical construction in 1 Kings when referring to Shimei:

> This verse uses *yom* (day) and the dual *muwth* just as Genesis 2:17 did. In On the day [*yom*] you go out and cross the brook Kidron, know for certain you shall surely [*muwth*]; die [*muwth*]; your blood shall be on your own head (1 Kings 2:37).

Genesis 2:17, *yom* referred to the action (eating) in the same way that *yom* refers to the action here (go out and cross over). In neither case do they mean that was the particular day that death would come, but the particular day they did what they weren't supposed to do.

Solomon also understood that it would not be a death on that particular day but that Shimei's days were numbered from that point. In other words, their (Adam and Shimei) actions on that day were what gave them the final death sentence — they would surely die as a result of their actions. Therefore, the day in Genesis 2:17 was referring to when Adam and the woman ate, not the day they died.

Was the Punishment Sleep, Instead of Physical Death?

Some people believe that the punishment was not really death, but that sleep (not deep sleep) entered the world at this time. Although this is not meant to be an exhaustive examination, I would lean against sleep being the punishment referred to in Genesis 2:17, since many other passages in the Bible describe sleep as a good thing. For example, sleep is pleasant in Ecclesiastes 5:12 and Jeremiah 31:26. The Lord often appeared to people while they were sleeping, and He Himself slept during a storm (Matthew 8:24; Mark 4:38; Luke 8:23). Also, Solomon's pronouncement against Shimei would not make any sense, as there is no doubt that Shimei already slept on a regular basis.

What is spoken of in Genesis 2:17 is a punishment and the foundation for Christ's physical death. If He merely had to sleep, then this undermines the reason for Christ's work on the Cross. Recall Romans 5:12: His death was a real death.

From a quick search, there are few passages referring to sleep as death in the Old Testament, such as Daniel 12:2 and Psalm 90:5, where much imagery is given in the context and so leads us to realize the metaphorical nature of the passages. For example, in the following verse in Daniel, those with insight will shine brightly. Obviously, it is not referring to a literal physical light emanating from humans. In the same figurative manner, people are compared to grass in Psalm 90:5.

The New Testament, written in Greek, does this as well. Jesus figuratively said that Lazarus was sleeping in John 11:11–13. The disciples failed to understand and took it as literal sleep, so Jesus had to correct them (John 11:14).

Regardless, this punishment was a real death, and Adam and Eve died — as will all the rest of us for our sins, which is all the more reason to receive Christ and be saved from death so that death will no longer have a sting (1 Corinthians 15:53–57).

18. How did defense/attack structures come about?

(This chapter was co-authored with Andy McIntosh and originally published in
The New Answers Book 1,[45] and reprinted here due to the relevant topic of the Fall.)

Many people question the goodness of God when they see "nature, red in tooth and claw,"[46] and therefore, they accuse those who believe in the Bible of not seeing reality in nature's fight for survival, which, in the view of the secular scientists, substantiates evolution.

In the past, many Bible-believers looked to nature as evidence of God's design in nature and attributed the features animals possessed to kill prey or defend themselves as all part of God's original design.

For example, in 1802 William Paley wrote the now-classic book *Natural Theology; or, Evidences of the Existence and Attributes of the Deity. Collected from the Appearances of Nature.* In this work, Paley makes the argument for the design in nature being attributed to a designer — God — and included features that were "red in tooth and claw" as part of this original design.

Darwin, who read Paley's work, realized that organisms have certain design features that make them fit for the environments in which they live. In other words, they were well designed for what they do — even the ability to cause pain, suffering, and death. However, Darwin later saw difficulties with Paley's argument concerning design. To Darwin, a creation capable of inflicting pain and death seemed to deny a good and loving Creator God.

Darwin could see that the idea of a benevolent designer did not square with the world that he observed. How could a good God be the author of death and bloodshed? The answer of Darwin and many others was to turn from the God of the Bible to a belief in man's ideas about the past that include millions of years of death and suffering.

A most notable adherent to this view in our present day is David Attenborough. Attenborough is the presenter of many popular nature

Figure 11. Eagles have pointed claws and sharp beaks.

documentaries produced by the British Broadcasting Corporation. In a similar journey to that of Darwin, he argues strongly for belief in evolution because of the suffering that the natural world exhibits. The quote below is very revealing as to what has moved Attenborough to an evolutionary position.

> When creationists talk about God creating every individual species as a separate act, they always instance hummingbirds, or orchids, sunflowers and beautiful things. But I tend to think instead of a parasitic worm that is boring through the eye of a boy sitting on the bank of a river in West Africa, [a worm] that's going to make him blind. And [I ask them], "Are you telling me that the God you believe in, who you also say is an all-merciful God, who cares for each one of us individually, are you saying that God created this worm that can live in no other way than in an innocent child's eyeball? Because that doesn't seem to me to coincide with a God who's full of mercy."[47]

The examples of Darwin and Attenborough show why the issue of defense/attack structures (DAS) is important, and how it is closely related to the existence of suffering and death in the world around us. Defense/attack structures include anything from claws and flesh-tearing beaks on birds of prey or the claws and teeth of cats, to a wasp's stinger or a poison dart frog's toxin.

What Are Some Defense/Attack Structures?

Examples of defense/attack structures are numerous in the world around us, existing in plants as well as animals. Let's look at a few.

Plant — Venus Flytrap

A great example in plants is the Venus flytrap. This plant snaps two of its lobes on any unsuspecting fly that ventures inside. The mechanism by which the trap snaps shut involves a complex interaction between elasticity, osmotic pressure in the cellular plant material, and growth. When the plant is open, the lobes are convex (bent outward), but when it is closed, the lobes are concave (forming a cavity). It is stable in both the open and closed positions, but it changes states to close quickly when triggered.[48]

Arachnid — Spider

A good example of DAS in the insect world is the spider. Spider webs are renowned for their potential to catch flying insects, such as flies and moths. The sophistication of silk production through special glands that keep the polymer soft right up until it is exuded behind the spider is still not understood.[49] Furthermore, the ability of the spider to make some strands sticky and others not, so that the spider itself only walks on the non-sticky parts is clearly a clever design feature. Not all spiders make webs, but they are all capable of producing silk in several varieties. Though the predatory nature of spiders is universal, the actual prey-catching technique of web-building is not the same for each species.

Insect — Bombardier Beetle

Another example in the insect world, and probably the most extraordinary, is the bombardier beetle. This insect possesses a sophisticated defense apparatus, which involves shooting a hot (212°F/100°C) noxious mixture of chemicals out of a special swivel nozzle in its backside, into the face of predators such as rodents, birds, frogs, or other insects.

Animals — Cats and Reptiles

Of the numerous examples of DAS in the animal world, the meat-eating lion, tiger, and other large cats (cheetah, lynx, etc.) would be the most obvious. It should be noted though that these creatures are not solely dependent on a carnivorous diet because there are known cases of large cats being able to survive on a vegetarian diet when meat has been not available in zoos.[50]

Figure 12. Alligator teeth are long and sharp.

Many animals in the reptile world also give us excellent examples of DAS. Chameleons have the ability to flick their tongues in only fractions of a second to capture their prey. Crocodiles and alligators have powerful jaws, and snakes possess poisonous fangs or deadly coils. The anaconda can kill bulls and tapirs easily with its extremely strong muscles.[51]

These are but a few of the DAS found around the world. If you check the plants and animals in your area, you can probably spot some of these and other defense/attack structures.

Why, Biblically, Is the World like This?

The biblical response to DAS is that the theology of Darwin and Attenborough has made a major assumption — the world is now what it always has been. The Bible, as early as Genesis 3, makes it clear that this is not the case.

The world (and indeed the universe) was originally perfect. Six times in Genesis 1 it states that what God had made was "good" and the seventh time that "God saw everything that He had made, and indeed it was very good" (Genesis 1:31). A perfect God would make nothing less. In fact, Moses, who also penned Genesis, declared in Deuteronomy 32:4 that all of God's works are perfect. The original creation was perfect, but we can see by looking at the world around us that there has been a drastic change. The change was a result of the Fall of man — an event that fundamentally altered the world.

The original world had no parasites boring into children's eyes or any other part of nature being "red in tooth and claw." The death and suffering in the past and in the present is a result of man's sin and rebellion against God. When the first man Adam disobeyed his Creator, all of creation was cursed, bringing disease, sickness, pain, suffering, and death into the world.

> Then to Adam He said, "Because you have heeded the voice of your wife, and have eaten from the tree of which I commanded you, saying, 'You shall not eat of it': cursed is the ground for your sake; in toil you shall eat of it all the days of your life. Both thorns and thistles it shall bring forth for you, and you shall eat the herb of the field. In the sweat of your face you shall eat bread till you return to the ground, for out of it you were taken; for dust you are, and to dust you shall return" (Genesis 3:17–19).

> To the woman He said, "I will greatly multiply your sorrow and your conception; in pain you shall bring forth children; your desire shall be for your husband, and he shall rule over you" (Genesis 3:16).

And earlier still, the Bible records what God spoke to the serpent: "So the LORD God said to the serpent: 'Because you have done this, you are cursed more than all cattle, and more than every beast of the field; on your belly you shall go, and you shall eat dust all the days of your life' " (Genesis 3:14). So in essence there were several changes at the Fall.

This is not just an Old Testament doctrine. The New Testament picks up on the inseparable connection between the world's state and man's condition. In Romans 8:22–23, Paul states, "For we know that the whole creation groans and labors with birth pangs together until now. Not only that, but we also who have the firstfruits of the Spirit, even we ourselves groan within ourselves, eagerly waiting for the adoption, the redemption of our body."

While the world has been cursed because of man's rebellion in Adam, there is coming a day — a day for the "redemption of our body" (Romans 8:23) — when at the resurrection of God's people, the world will also be liberated from the Curse. In Romans 8, Paul makes it clear that the extent of this Curse encompasses the whole creation.

Table 2. Effects of the Curse in Genesis 3

Verse	Some of the known effects	Said to
Genesis 3:14	1. Serpent cursed *more than* other animals — specifically mentions crawling on its belly and eating dust. 2. Other animals are cursed; to what extent, we aren't told.	Serpent
Genesis 3:16	1. Increased pain and sorrow in childbearing and raising children. 2. Their desire will be for their husbands.	Woman/ Eve
Genesis 3:17–19	1. Ground is cursed — specifically mentions thorns and thistles and the pain and sorrow associated with working the ground. We aren't told the other effects of the Curse. 2. Death — man would return to dust.	Man/ Adam

When we look at defense/attack structures in the animal or plant kingdom, we must look at them in the context of a biblical theology. Let's review the clear teachings from Scripture.

1. Man and animals were originally created as vegetarian (Genesis 1:29–30). Throughout Genesis 1 the Lord states repeatedly that the created order was "good" and then in Genesis 1:31, "very good." Thus, "nature, red in tooth and claw" was not part of God's original creation.

In verse 30, God explicitly states, "Also, to every beast of the earth, to every bird of the air, and to everything that creeps on the earth, in which there is life, I have given every green herb for food." Literally in the Hebrew, the phrase "in which there is life" is *nephesh chayyah*. This phrase is translated "living soul" and is used in Genesis 1:20–21 and Genesis 2:7 when referring to man and animals. However, this phrase is never used in reference to plants (or invertebrates), thus highlighting the difference between plant life and human and animal life.

The Curse in Genesis 3 caused a major change in both animals and plants. The animals were cursed — Genesis 3:14 says, "You are cursed *more than all cattle*, and *more than every beast of the field*" (emphasis added). The plants were also cursed — Genesis 3:17–18 says, "Cursed is the ground for your sake; in toil you shall eat of it all the days of your life. Both thorns and thistles it shall bring forth for you, and you shall eat the herb of the field." (There is evidence that thorns are formed from altered leaves.[52])

2. It was not until after the Flood that God allowed man to eat meat (Genesis 1:29–30, 9:3). Later in Scripture the prophet Isaiah refers to a future time when there will be a reverse of the Curse: "The wolf also shall dwell with the lamb, the leopard shall lie down with the young goat, the calf and the young lion and the fatling together; and a little child shall lead them" (Isaiah 11:6). " 'The wolf and the lamb shall feed together, the lion shall eat straw like the ox, and dust shall be the serpent's food. They shall not hurt nor destroy in all My holy mountain,' says the LORD" (Isaiah 65:25).

3. The Book of Revelation speaks of a time when the Curse will be removed (Revelation 22:3) and there will be no more pain, suffering, or death (Revelation 21:4).

The Bible provides us with a big picture as we look at defense/attack structures.

Two Major Perspectives to Understand DAS Biblically

Two primary alternatives can easily explain defense/attack structures from a biblical perspective: (1) the present features used in defense and attack were not originally used for that purpose, and (2) the DAS design features were brought in by God *as a result of* the Fall.

The first perspective — that the present features were not originally used for defense/attack purposes — indicates that DAS were used for different functions before the Fall. Another way to clarify this perspective is to say that the design was the same but the function was different.

Let's take sharp teeth as an example. When people see animals with sharp teeth, they most commonly interpret this to mean that

Figure 13. Sin brought changes such as death, suffering, and carnivory into the world.

the animal is a meat-eater. When scientists find fossils of creatures with sharp teeth, they also interpret this to mean that the animal was a meat-eater. But is this a proper interpretation? Not really. Sharp teeth in animals indicate only one thing — the animal has sharp teeth.

Creatures with sharp teeth do not necessarily use them to rip other animals apart today. For example, the giant panda has very sharp teeth, yet it eats entirely bamboo shoots. Also, the fruit bat, which at first might appear to have teeth consistent with a carnivorous diet, eats primarily fruit. The Bible teaches that animals were created to be vegetarian (Genesis 1:30), so we must be careful not to merely assume what an animal ate based on its teeth.

Figure 14. Bears have sharp teeth, but they eat many vegetarian meals.

Other DAS can also be explained in this way. Claws could have been used to grip vegetarian foods or branches for climbing. And chameleon tongues could have been used to reach out and grab vegetarian foods, etc. This perspective has the advantage of never having to suggest that God designed a structure or system feature to be harmful to another living creature of His creation.

It is evident that for the silk-producing structure in spiders, it is hard to establish an alternative function for these glands, though spiders have been shown to catch and eat pollen.[53] The evidence seems to point to such structures being designed as they are to effectively catch things like insects. However, we may simply not know the original harmless function of these structures.

Consequently, many have suggested the fact that some creatures have continued to eat plants, which actually indicates that predatory habits came due to altered function. Bears commonly eat vegetarian foods. There have been lions and vultures documented to refuse eating meat.[54]

Even viruses (genetic carriers that infect a host with almost always deleterious results) may have originally been used in a different and beneficial role before the Fall. In a similar manner, harmful bacteria may have had a different and better purpose than their current function.

However, this perspective does have some shortcomings, especially when we apply it to the whole of DAS. One such problem is that of thorns. It can be argued that trees, bushes, etc., use thorns solely as a defense mechanism. But the Bible indicates that thorns and thistles came as a result of the Fall (Genesis 3:17–19). So something indeed changed at the Curse.

Thorns and Thistles

This first perspective avoids God designing DAS in a perfect world for the purpose of harming something that was alive.

The second perspective — DAS design features were brought in by God *as a result of* the Fall — calls for design alterations after the Fall to allow such attack and defense structures. To clarify, this was the result of man's sin, not God's original design, and the consequences of sin still remain. Such "cursed design" is from God's intelligence as a punishment for the man's, the woman's, and the serpent's disobedience. This second perspective would then better explain some things like sharp teeth, claws, the special glands that make the spider silk, etc.

There is some warrant for this view in Scripture since we know that plants have been made such that now some of them have thorns (physically changed form) and that the serpent changed form to crawl on its belly (physically changed form). Since there was a physical change and this was passed along to offspring, then there had to be genetic alterations. Some of these changes could have been immediate, and others could have been slower in revealing themselves.

Regardless, the genetic blueprint of these systems must have changed such that DAS became evident. Remembering that God knows the future, it is possible that under this scenario the devices were placed latently in the genetic code of these creatures at creation and were "turned on" at the Fall.

Another possibility is that God redesigned the creatures after the Fall to have such features as DAS in them. Thus, the latter possibility still allows for the existence of such latent features in the design still being "very good." However, since defense/attack structures are a reminder of a sin-cursed world full of death and suffering, it was more likely changed at the Fall as opposed to being simply dormant.

Scripture that gives implied support to this perspective is that after the Fall man would know pain and hard work and would eventually die

(Genesis 3:19). Some biological change is experienced. Pain and sorrow in childbirth are a direct result of the Fall, and the serpent is radically redesigned after his rebellion. So this overall position may be the better of the two, though we wouldn't be dogmatic.

Conclusion

Both biblical perspectives explain the changes that occurred when man sinned and the world fell from a perfect one to an imperfect one, and both positions have merits. But the Bible doesn't specifically say one way or another. In fact, there could be aspects of both perspectives that may have happened. Not all creatures with DAS need to be explained in the same way. For some it may have been that their existing functions adapted, while there seems to be every indication that other mechanisms came in after the Fall.

Regardless, the accusation that a loving and perfect God made the world as we see it today ignores the Bible's teachings about the results of the Curse. A proper understanding of why there are defense/attack structures in the world today should be a reminder that the world is sin-cursed and that we are all sinners in need of a Savior.

After the Fall, God acted justly. He did what was right. But during the curses in Genesis 3, God did something that only a loving God would do — He gave the first prophecy of redemption. He promised a Savior. Genesis 3:15 says, "And I will put enmity between you and the woman, and between your seed and her Seed; He shall bruise your head, and you shall bruise His heel."

The One who would crush the head of the serpent would be born of a virgin, the seed of a woman. This is the first of many prophecies of Jesus Christ coming as the seed of a woman — a virgin birth. It was truly a loving and gracious God who came to earth in the form of a man and died for us and paid the penalty of our sins on the Cross.

DAS should remind us that when God says something, it will come to pass. When people receive Christ as their Savior, they will one day enjoy eternal life in a world that no longer has any curse or death or suffering or pain (Revelation 21:4, 22:3).

> For God so loved the world that He gave His only begotten Son, that whoever believes in Him should not perish but have everlasting life. For God did not send His Son into the world to condemn the world, but that the world through Him might be saved. He who believes in Him is not condemned; but he who does not believe is condemned already, because he has not believed in the name of the only begotten Son of God (John 3:16–18).

19. Did Adam and Eve have to sleep before the Fall?

The Bible doesn't tell us much about the world before the Fall. But we can make a few inferences based on what God has given us.

> So the LORD God caused a deep sleep [Strong's 08639] to fall on Adam, and he slept; and He took one of his ribs, and closed up the flesh in its place (Genesis 2:21).

The word used here means specifically a deep sleep (Hebrew: *tardemah*, Strong's number 08639). This implies that normal sleep probably did exist, and this deep sleep is much more than normal sleep (as a side note, this gives us a basis for sleep during surgical procedures). So I suspect Adam and Eve did have some sort of regular sleep cycle.

However, I wouldn't be certain, as Adam and Eve could have been created merely with the capability to sleep initially. They may not have needed it. Perhaps sleep, after the Fall, helps recoup a little of what was lost, since man no longer had access to the tree of life after sin (Genesis 3:22).

In particular, I suspect sleep was a part of the original creation as a reminder of what God did during creation week. God, at the end of His work of creation, rested. Later, Moses presented the Israelites with the Ten Commandments, and in Exodus 20:11, God points out that the basis for God resting was a pattern for man to follow. So man was created to rest — even before the Fall. Also, since God created night during creation week, it would be logical that Adam and Eve would have needed rest and sleep before the Fall.

Today, in our fallen world, proper amounts of sleep often refresh the mind and the body. While there's no definitive proof Adam and Eve slept prior to the Fall, rest — in the form of sleep — seems to have been part of the original creation. But take the time to examine the issue yourself.

20. If Adam knew of good and evil, because he was programmed with language, then why did God create the tree of the knowledge of good and evil?

There is a difference between knowing the definition of what good and evil are and *experiencing* it. Let me explain in more detail.

Adam would be able to "understand" the concept of evil without having "experienced" it. Also, when discussing death/die with Adam, he easily knew what it was since God preprogrammed language into him and he was able to speak to God and with Eve right from the start.

With regard to Adam and Eve *experiencing* death and evil, it came with sin. One thing is the confusion over the word "knowledge." Adam would be able to understand the concept of evil and death without having experienced it.

Recall that in Genesis 4:1 Adam "knew" his wife and conceived a son — this was *experiential*:

> Now Adam knew Eve his wife, and she conceived and bore Cain, and said, "I have acquired a man from the LORD" (Genesis 4:1).

Obviously, Adam understood who his wife was and even named her, but the word "knew" means *to experience* in Hebrew. The same word for "knew" is the same word used as "know" as in Genesis 3:22:

> Then the LORD God said, "Behold, the man has become like one of Us, to know good and evil. And now, lest he put out his hand and take also of the tree of life, and eat, and live forever."

In fact, the word "knowledge" as in the "tree of the knowledge of good and evil," is a derivation of this same word (Hebrew: *da'ath*, Strong's 01847).

Mankind's experience with evil became different. Once they sinned, Adam and Eve became subject to evil. John MacArthur put it this way:

> In the original creation, God knew evil in the same way as an oncologist knows about cancer — not by personal experience but by knowledge about it (in God's case, by foreknowledge). But after Adam and Eve sinned, they knew evil in the same way as a cancer sufferer knows cancer — by sad personal experience.[55]

Therefore, it is likely that they understood what evil was, but when they ate they became subjected to and experienced it — slaves to sin, bondage to sin.

21. If God is holy and good, why is the world unholy and fallen?

Part of the problem in understanding this lies in our view of holiness (i.e., separation, perfection). Unholiness is the absence of holiness. That may seem obvious, but I'll unpack the statement.

To be succinct, "holiness" must exist for there to be "unholiness," which is the absence of holiness. Therefore, "unholiness" can't exist without "holiness."

When God created the universe, everything *was* holy. God said it was "perfect/very good" in Genesis 1:31 (see also Deuteronomy 32:4). However, it would be a fallacy to assume that things would remain holy considering that man had the power of contrite choice, as did angels when they were created (i.e., man was permitted to "freely" eat).[56]

While God is holy and has an unchanging nature (Malachi 3:5), other created beings, including humans and angels (see Ezekiel 28:15), can fall from a holy state to an unholy state through sin — this is very similar to the confusion about whether something that is "perfect" can ever become imperfect. Of course, God is perfect and cannot become imperfect. But His creatures can, as Ezekiel 28:15 shows us. The misunderstanding comes from equivocating on the word "perfect." Webster's first definition for the word refers to something without fault or defect, which could apply to God or the original state of His creation. The third definition would only apply to God in that He is lacking in no essential detail and, as a result, cannot fall from perfection.

So, really the question should be: how can something unholy ever be restored to a perfectly holy state? It cannot be done of oneself. We need the help of the One who is perfectly holy. Only Jesus Christ, who is the perfect and holy God, can restore mankind to a holy state (2 Corinthians 5:21).

22. Shouldn't Eve have been a clone of Adam?

When we look at the woman (Eve), we find that God took the rib/ side (Hebrew: *tsela*), but built a new person — with new DNA and all. I can say with confidence that we know that Eve wasn't a clone because she was female. She had different sex chromosomes (XX) as opposed to Adam's (XY).

If she had the same DNA, they would have both been males. So God stepped in and specially created Eve — as well as her DNA — to be just as unique as Adam's. This means they were both special creations and both made in the image of God, since Eve came from Adam. Thus, God ingrained the vast majority of information that appears in various people groups today — right from the start.

23. Did Abel eat the meat of the sacrifice?

Was Abel eating meat soon after the Curse even though he wasn't supposed to (Genesis 1:29)? After all, he kept the flocks and sacrificed an animal in Genesis 4:2–4, and it wasn't until Genesis 9:3 that humanity was permitted to eat meat.

Matthew indicates that Abel was righteous and therefore was not being disobedient to God's command to be vegetarian in Genesis 1:29.

> . . . that on you may come all the righteous blood shed on the earth, from the blood of righteous Abel to the blood of Zechariah, son of Berechiah, whom you murdered between the temple and the altar (Matthew 23:35).

So as to why Abel was tending flocks, we need to consider that flocks can yield many other things besides food — such as wool, milk, leather, etc. A fattened lamb, for example, would produce a great deal of wool, had the most life ahead of it, and so on; hence, it was the most valuable.

So when Abel sacrificed the fattened ones, he was offering his best — a true blood sacrifice. This sacrifice was acceptable to the Lord, as it mimicked what God did in making a blood sacrifice to cover Adam and Eve's sins (see Hebrews 9:22 and Genesis 3:21).

The passage doesn't indicate that Abel *ate* of the sacrifice, so there is no reason to assume he did. When God sacrificed animals to cover Adam and Eve's sin, there is no indication that they ate either. Since Abel mimicked what God did, then there is no reason to believe that he would have eaten from the sacrifice.

The first possibility of righteously eating the sacrifice would have been with Noah and his family after the Flood. When they sacrificed, God told them they were no longer restricted to a vegetarian diet (Genesis 8:20–9:3).

24. When did Adam and Eve rebel?

In Genesis 1:28, God commanded Adam and Eve to be fruitful and multiply. If they had waited very long, they would have been sinning against God by not being fruitful. Also, since they were created with perfect bodies, it would not have taken long for Eve to conceive. So the time between the creation and the Fall must have been short.

Some people have said that the Fall could not have occurred so early because Adam walked with God in the Garden and this suggests an intimate relationship between Adam and His Creator that could only be developed *over time*. However, the Bible never says that Adam walked with God in the Garden. Although many people have taught this, it is not found in Scripture. Adam and Eve were hiding because of their sin when they heard the sound of the Lord God walking in the Garden (Genesis 3:8), *and note* that this is after sin.

In Genesis 3, Adam and Eve sinned (in part due to Satan's actions) and were kicked out of the Garden of Eden. According to Scripture, this happened prior to conceiving their first child, Cain (Genesis 4:1).

Genesis 5:3 indicates that Adam had Seth at age 130 and Genesis 4:25 indicates this took place after Cain killed Abel. Adam had at least three children before Seth: Cain (Genesis 4:1), Cain's wife[57] (Genesis 4:17), and Abel (Genesis 4:2). Since Cain and Abel were old enough to work with crops and herds, respectively, the maximum time before the Fall would have to be much less than 130 years.

Looking back at the creation week, Adam and Eve couldn't have sinned on day 6 (the day Adam and the woman were created), since God declared that everything was "very good." Otherwise, sin would be very good. Day 7 is also unlikely, since God sanctified that day. Therefore, the Fall likely happened soon after this.

Archbishop Ussher suggests that Adam sinned on the tenth day of the first month in Ussher's chronology, which is the Day of Atonement.[58] The Day of Atonement presumably represents the first sacrifice, which God made by killing animals (from which He made coats of skins in Genesis 3:21) to cover Adam and Eve's sin.

Ussher's reasons for choosing this date make sense. However, we can't be certain of the exact date or length of time prior to the Fall beyond the points established above.

25. How long ago was the Curse?

The Curse would have been fairly soon after the creation of Adam and Eve on day 6 because it didn't take long for them to sin (see *When did Adam and Eve rebel?*). We can do a basic calculation to arrive at the date of creation and Adam's creation. The Curse must have been close to the same time. So let's calculate the date of creation.

Adam was created on day 6, so there were five days before him. If we add up the dates from Adam to Abraham, we get about 2,000 years, using the Masoretic Hebrew text (which is the standard Hebrew text that most English translations are based on) of Genesis 5 and 11.[59] Whether Christian or secular, most scholars would agree that Abraham lived about 2,000 B.C. (4,000 years ago).

So a simple calculation is:

$$\begin{array}{r} 5 \text{ days} \\ + 2{,}000 \text{ years} \\ + 4{,}000 \text{ years} \\ \hline \char"7E\; 6{,}000 \text{ years} \end{array}$$

At this point, the first five days are negligible. Quite a few people have done this calculation using the Masoretic text and, with careful attention to the biblical details, arrived at the same time frame of about 6,000 years, or about 4000 B.C. Two of the most popular, and perhaps the best, are a recent work by Dr. Floyd Jones and a much earlier book by Archbishop James Ussher (1581–1656):

Table 3. Jones and Ussher

	Who?	Age calculated	Reference and date
1	Archbishop James Ussher	4004 B.C.	*The Annals of the World,* A.D. 1658[60]
2	Dr. Floyd Nolan Jones	4004 B.C.	*The Chronology of the Old Testament,* A.D. 1993[61]

Often there is a misconception that Ussher and Jones were the only ones to do a chronology and arrive at an age of about 6,000 years. However, this is not the case. Jones gives a listing of several chronologists who undertook the task of calculating the age of the earth based on the Bible, and their calculations range from 5501 to 3836 B.C. A few are listed in table 2.

Table 4. Chronologists' calculations according to Dr. Jones[62]

	Chronologist	When calculated?	Date B.C.
1	Julius Africanus	c. 240	5501
2	George Syncellus	c. 810	5492
3	John Jackson	1752	5426
4	Dr. William Hales	c. 1830	5411
5	Eusebius	c. 330	5199
6	Marianus Scotus	c. 1070	4192
7	L. Condomanus	n/a	4141
8	Thomas Lydiat	c. 1600	4103
9	M. Michael Maestlinus	c. 1600	4079
10	J. Ricciolus	n/a	4062
11	Jacob Salianus	c. 1600	4053
12	H. Spondanus	c. 1600	4051
13	Martin Anstey	1913	4042
14	W. Lange	n/a	4041
15	E. Reinholt	n/a	4021
16	J. Cappellus	c. 1600	4005
17	E. Greswell	1830	4004
18	E. Faulstich	1986	4001
19	D. Petavius	c. 1627	3983
20	Frank Klassen	1975	3975
21	Becke	n/a	3974
22	Krentzeim	n/a	3971
23	W. Dolen	2003	3971
24	E. Reusnerus	n/a	3970

25	J. Claverius	n/a	3968
26	C. Longomontanus	c. 1600	3966
27	P. Melanchthon	c. 1550	3964
28	J. Haynlinus	n/a	3963
29	A. Salmeron	d. 1585	3958
30	J. Scaliger	d. 1609	3949
31	M. Beroaldus	c. 1575	3927
32	A. Helwigius	c. 1630	3836

As you will likely note from table 2, the dates are not all 4004 B.C. There are several reasons chronologists have different dates,[63] but the two primary ones are:

- Some used the Septuagint or another early translation instead of the Hebrew Masoretic text. The Septuagint is a Greek translation of the Hebrew Old Testament done about 250 B.C. by about 70 Jewish scholars (which is why it is often called the LXX, the Roman numeral for 70). While good in most places, there are a number of inaccuracies. For example, one relates to the Genesis chronologies in which the LXX calculations would have Methuselah living beyond the Flood — without being on the ark!

- Several points in the biblical time-line are not straightforward to calculate. They require very careful study of more than one passage. These include exactly how much time the Israelites were in Egypt and what Terah's age was when Abraham was born. (See Jones's and Ussher's books for a detailed discussion of these difficulties.)

The first four in table 2 have much higher dates and are calculated from the Septuagint, which gives ages for the patriarchs' firstborn much higher than the Masoretic text or the Samarian Pentateuch (another version from the Jews in Samaria just before Christ). Because of this, the

LXX adds in extra time. Though the Samarian and Masoretic texts are much closer, they still have a couple of differences.

Table 5. Septuagint, Masoretic, and Samarian early patriarchal ages[64]

Name	Masoretic	Samarian Pentateuch	Septuagint
Adam	130	130	230
Seth	105	105	205
Enosh	90	90	190
Cainan	70	70	170
Mahalaleel	65	65	165
Jared	162	62	162
Enoch	65	65	165
Methuselah	187	67	167
Lamech	182	53	188
Noah	500	500	500

Using data from table 2 (excluding the Septuagint calculations and including Jones and Ussher), the average date of the creation of the earth is 4045 B.C. This yields an average of about 6,000 years for the time of the Curse.

The world has been enduring the results of the Curse for 6,000 years and there are still many remnants of beauty and wonder. Just imagine what it was like before sin and what believers can look forward to in the new heavens and new earth where there is no more Curse.

26. Wasn't the Curse and death a good thing to keep the earth from being overpopulated?

Human Overpopulation?

Since God knows the future, He knew Adam and Eve would sin. This explains why He already had a plan in place to redeem fallen man. The first prophecy of Christ comes in Genesis 3:15, which states that He will come as the seed of a woman/virgin birth (see also Isaiah 7:14). If you look closely at Genesis 2:17, God foreknew that mankind would sin: "For in the day you eat of it." He didn't say, "If you eat of it."

Theoretically, let's say that sin did not happen — no original sin happened, the human population exploded, and people filled the earth. Pay close attention to what God said: *fill* the earth, not *overpopulate* it.[65] The command was to populate until the earth was full, and then reproduction would most likely cease. Similar statements govern sea creatures (Genesis 1:22). Consider if someone asked me to fill up a glass of water. Would I fill it and then keep putting water in it so that it overflowed? No, I would fill it only until it was full. The word *fill* basically places limits on humans right from the start. Nonetheless, if sin never entered the world, then there is no reason to assume God wouldn't have said "stop reproducing" once humans had filled the earth. Remember, in a world without sin, God's relationship with mankind wouldn't be tarnished; hence, open communication should still be there.

God can and does change some civil rules from time to time. For example, originally we could only be vegetarian (Genesis 1:29), but after the Flood, God gave man permission to eat meat (Genesis 9:3). Also, there used to be rigorous sacrificial laws, but now they are done away with due to Christ's perfect sacrifice. But such changes happen in our sin-cursed world.

After the Flood, Genesis 9:1 and Genesis 9:8 reaffirm that man was to reproduce and multiply and fill the earth as well. The basis for overpopulation comes from uniformitarianism and projecting current growth rates into the future. Uniformitarianism has failed in the fields of geology and radiometric dating while looking at the past. So, why trust the results of uniformitarianism here? We can be sure that God knew humanity would sin. To deny this would be to deny that God knows the future, even though He declared that He tells the end from the beginning (Isaiah 46:10).

Animal Overpopulation?

From Genesis 1:22 and Genesis 1:28, we can infer that man and sea creatures may have had lower initial populations so that there would be plenty of room to multiply. With humans, there were only two people to start with: Adam and Eve. Birds were to multiply but *not* commanded to fill the earth, so it seems they may never have filled the earth before their reproduction would have ceased in a perfect world. But they must have had room to multiply, too. Regardless, sin entered into the world, so such "what if" questions are mere speculation.

Land animals were not commanded to multiply or fill the earth in Genesis 1. I would suggest that this implies land animals were created in more abundance — with little or no necessity to reproduce in great quantities in a perfect creation.[66] After sin, though, this became a necessity, since death began reigning in animals. The first recorded death of an animal was the one used to cover Adam and the woman's sin (coats of skins in Genesis 3:21). Later in the Bible, we find that land animals on the ark were told to multiply abundantly after the Flood, which had caused a massive worldwide graveyard of previous animals (Genesis 8:17). Since there were no land-dwelling, air-breathing animals (Genesis 7:22) on the earth after the Flood (except for those in the ark), this makes sense — their populations were low for this new starting point. These land animals were not told to fill the earth, but at this point they lived in a sin-cursed world where death reigns, so an upper limit may have been unnecessary.

So *no*, the Curse would have been irrelevant to overpopulation in a perfect world. We need to remember why there is a curse (i.e., because of sin).

27. Questions about the tree of life

Did Adam and Eve Have to Eat from the Tree of Life to Keep from Dying?

This question assumes that the man and woman were already dying and required the tree of life to live. But there is no reason to assume they were, as death was the punishment for sin (Genesis 2:17) and they hadn't sinned yet.

> And the LORD God commanded the man, "You are free to eat from any tree in the garden; but you must not eat from the tree of the knowledge of good and evil, for when you eat of it you will surely die" (Genesis 2:16–17; NIV).

Adam and Eve probably could have eaten from the tree of life originally (Genesis 2:16), but God gives no decree that they had to eat of it to sustain their life at that point. However, the tree may have been one means by which God used to help support and maintain Adam and Eve — perhaps a type of sustenance. God ultimately sustains all things (Colossians 1:17), and if we look at the Israelites wandering in the desert for 40 years while their feet never swelled and their clothes never wore out (Deuteronomy 29:5), we see a glimpse of what God can do. The fruit or leaves of the tree of life were not required for the Israelites in this case.

Also, keep in mind that the Bible gives no hints that they had to eat of this tree until after sin. After they sinned in Genesis 3, God sentenced them to die as per Genesis 2:17 (Genesis 3:19), and this was in part why they were forbidden to take from the tree of life. But consider God's statement here:

> Then the LORD God said, "Behold, the man has become like one of Us, knowing good and evil; and now, he might stretch out

his hand, and take also from the tree of life, and eat, and live forever" (Genesis 3:22; NASB).

This seems to imply that Adam and Eve could have eaten from the tree of life after they sinned to live forever. Had they been permitted to eat from the tree of life, then they would have been forced to live eternally in a sin-cursed world. But God had a better plan in place — one of redemption in Jesus Christ with a new heavens and new earth that would not be cursed.

God is the only Savior (Psalm 62:6; John 14:6), and through Him is the only way to live forever. Thus, God stopped them from trying to attain eternal life in a sin-cursed world. God demonstrated His grace in refusing to allow mankind to live eternally in a world filled with sorrow and suffering. Instead, He has provided the way for us to enjoy eternal life in a place where there is no more death, sorrow, pain, or Curse (Revelation 21:3–4, 22:3).

Expositor John Gill made some interesting points about the tree of life:

> . . . set there as in the most excellent place, where it might be most conspicuous, and to be come at; for before Adam sinned, as there was no prohibition of his eating of it, so there was no obstruction to it; and as he had a grant to eat of it, with the other trees, it was designed for his use, to support and maintain his natural life, which would have been continued, had he persisted in his obedience and state of innocence, and very probably by means of this chiefly: hence the son of Sirach calls it the tree of immortality,

> The knowledge of the commandments of the Lord is
> the doctrine of life: and they that do things that please
> him shall receive the fruit of the tree of immortality.
> (Sirach 19:19)

and it might be also a sign, token, and symbol to him of his dependence on God; that he received his life from him; and that this was preserved by his blessing and providence, and not by his own power and skill; and that this would be continued, provided he transgressed not the divine law: and it seems to have a further respect, even to eternal life; by Christ; for though it might not be a symbol of that life to Adam in his state of innocence, yet it became so after his fall: hence Christ is sometimes signified by the tree of life, #Pr 3:18 Re 2:7 who is not only the author of natural and spiritual life, but the giver of eternal life; the promise of it is in him, and the blessing itself; he has made way for it by his obedience, sufferings, and death, and is the way unto it; it is in his gift, and he bestows it on all his people, and it will lie greatly in the enjoyment of him. The situation of this tree in the midst of the garden well agrees with him who is in the midst of his church and people, #Re 1:13 2:7 stands open, is in sight, and is accessible to them all now, who may come to him, and partake of the fruits and blessings of his grace, which are many, constant, and durable, #Re 22:2 and who will be seen and enjoyed by all, to all eternity.[67]

Apparently, the fruit and leaves of the tree of life will be consumed in heaven (Revelation 2:7, 22:2, 22:14). This is something to look forward to.

Why Didn't God Remove the Tree of Life from the Garden?

I suggest that the banishment of man was not just because of the tree of life, but also to till the ground outside the garden. Part of the punishment was to work the ground by the sweat of the brow (Genesis 3:19). The garden was already perfectly prepared by God with fruits and would be easy to maintain.

Adam and Eve rose up their own thoughts by deciding for themselves if God's command not to eat was true; they were, in essence, claiming to be equal to God. And notice that they were kicked out of the garden and

Figure 15. The fruit and leaves of the tree of life as depicted in the Creation Museum

Adam was told to work the ground by the sweat of his brow (Genesis 3:19-23). In other words, the Lord basically said to *go till, plant, and maintain your own garden* since they wanted to be like God.

But we can't ignore another incredible implications. If the man ate from the tree of life, he would live forever in a sinful state and sin-cursed universe. Such a punishment would mean no possibility of salvation to live in a new heavens and new earth without sin — one absent of pain (Revelation 21–22).

In fact, we read that in heaven the tree's leaves will be used for healing. Perhaps, in the Garden of Eden, it would have performed a similar function. In today's world, we find that plants often have some healing properties (e.g., aloe). It may simply be that God created the tree of life with the particular effects to help heal from the impact of aging that would lead to death (hence, living forever).

What Happened to the Tree of Life? Did the Flood Destroy It?

Nowhere in the early passages of Genesis do we read that anyone tried to force their way back into the Garden of Eden to get to the tree of life. One would presume that even descendants of Adam and Eve would have lived forever had they eaten from the tree of life as well.[68] Considering how long most people lived before the Flood (at least the ones recorded in Genesis 5), the pre-Flood population may not have been as interested in prolonging their lives as we would be with our shorter post-Flood life spans.

The Flood of Noah's day was more than likely the event that annihilated both the Garden of Eden and its contents. It would be at this time that the cherubim would no longer need to guard the path to the tree of life. Also, keep in mind that God did not declare that trees/plants (or even marine life) would all be preserved (like land animals that breath through the nostrils — Genesis 6:18–20, 7:21–23).[69] So extinction could have been a possibility with a variety of kinds — perhaps including both the tree of life and the tree of the knowledge of good and evil.

However, one needs to be careful here, too. There are other possibilities that we may have overlooked. For example, in a sin-cursed world, things rarely stay the same. With the Curse, God no longer upholds the universe perfectly and things run down and have problems. As a result, we are in a world full of detrimental mutations that have been killing off living things. With natural selection and mutations, the offspring of the tree of life could have lost the ability to heal. In light of this, if the tree of life does still exist today, it could be so degraded that we would not recognize it, nor would its effects be what they were originally.

More About the Tree of Life

It is true that the tree of life is in heaven, but I would still lean against the tree simply being transplanted to heaven. If this were the case, then why did God place the cherubim to guard the way to it on earth? Also, in Genesis 3, God cursed the ground due to man's sin. This curse directly affected vegetation (e.g., thorns and thistles). This particular aspect was brought out specifically. The Lord surely revealed this to us, knowing full-well that He would wear a crown of thorns at the time of his crucifixion.

Regardless, the vegetation was a recipient of this curse to the ground (for their very roots grow in the ground). So this means that the curse affected the tree of life that was in the Garden. With this in mind, consider that nothing *unclean, defiled, or impure* will ever enter into heaven as per Revelation 21:27 (even people must be made clean and pure through Christ's blood to enter). So it makes more sense that the tree of life in heaven was created in heaven.

Further to this, in heaven, there is more than one tree of life (one on each side of the river) in Revelation 22:2. Yet there was only one mentioned in the Garden.

28. Were Satan and the angels (or other heavenly host) created in the "image of God"?

The Image of God

Being made in the image of God is a major factor distinguishing humanity from the animals and other physical entities. In Genesis 1:26–27, we read:

> Then God said, "Let Us make man in Our image, according to Our likeness; let them have dominion over the fish of the sea, over the birds of the air, and over the cattle, over all the earth and over every creeping thing that creeps on the earth." So God created man in His own image; in the image of God He created him; male and female He created them.

According to verse 27, both Adam and the woman (male and female) were created in the image of God. Since we are all descendants of our first parents, then we have been made in the image of God as well. Genesis 9:6 confirms that the image of God is passed on to Adam's descendants. What sets us apart from animals and plants is that we have a spiritual aspect. Plants have a "body," or at least a physical aspect, but no soul.

This is why creationists often point out that plants are not living in the biblical sense. Animals, on the other hand, were created with a body and a soul (Hebrew: *nephesh*) according to such passages as Genesis 1:24–25. Unlike animals, humanity has a spiritual aspect as well.[70] Paul's letter to the Thessalonians says:

> Now may the God of peace Himself sanctify you completely; and may your whole spirit, soul, and body be preserved blameless at the coming of our Lord Jesus Christ (1 Thessalonians 5:23).

Mankind has a unique spiritual aspect, and this spirit is uniquely made in the image of God.[71] We should expect this image to have certain aspects of God's characteristics since God is spirit (John 4:24). However, this does not mean that we have all of them, for we have but a taste of God's attributes. This image was first placed into Adam when God breathed life into him.

> And the LORD God formed man of the dust of the ground, and breathed into his nostrils the breath [spirit] of life; and man became a living being (Genesis 2:7).

The Hebrew word for *breath* here is *nashamah* and is often translated as "breath" or "spirit." Christians often describe the image of God as superior intellectual ability, such as reason and abstract thought, worship of God, language and communication with God, ability to make decisions, creative expression, immortality, and emotions such as love, sadness, anger, and so on. These attributes show how separate man is from beasts and other physical entities; however, angels, Satan, demons, and other heavenly host have many of these same attributes.

Spiritual Beings . . . Image of God, Too?

One may quickly dismiss such an intriguing question without much thought by claiming that the Bible doesn't say angels were created with the "image of God." However, a quick dismissal may be unwise. After all, the Scriptures do not say they *weren't* created with the image of God either. The Bible doesn't give us extensive background about angels since its focus is on mankind, but we can examine what it does tell us about angels in attempting to answer this question.

Consider a few of these characteristics and see how Scripture ascribes them to spiritual beings. While many examples can be found in Scripture, a couple should suffice for each.

• *Superior intellectual ability such as reason and abstract thought*

When the serpent, which was influenced by Satan, deceived Eve in Genesis 3, there was considerable intellectual ability, even being termed "clever/cunning." Satan, referring to Job in Job 1:9–11 and Job 2:4–5, used logic to say that Job would turn if he lost his possessions and became diseased. (Many people in such a situation probably would have turned from God, but God knew Job would not.)

• Worship of God

Hebrews 1:6 points out that angels worship the Lord. We also see the heavenly host praising God in Luke 2:13–14.

• Language and communication with God

Satan was able to converse with God in Job 1–2. Satan was also able to understand Christ (Mark 8:33). The legion of demons spoke with Christ (Mark 5:9). Angels often spoke to people, for example, Mary, the mother of Christ, and John in Revelation.

• Ability to make decisions

Satan and the demons obviously fell from grace when sinning against God.

• Creative expression

The four living creatures (whom are among the heavenly host) in Revelation 5:8–10 played harps and sang a new song. With the extensive amount of praise and worship to God by the angels and heavenly host, we would expect them to create much music — even the morning stars (i.e., angels) sang for joy at the creation (Job 38:7).

• Immortality

Like humans, eternal life will be the outcome of angels who did not fall and eternal punishment for Satan and his angels (Matthew 25:41; Revelation 20:10).

• Emotions such as love, joy, desire, sadness, pride, and anger

Luke 15:10 indicates that angels are joyous when one person repents. The devil has great wrath in Revelation 12:12. The angels and the devil have desires (1 Peter 1:12; John 8:44).

Conclusion

Since the Bible doesn't say whether spiritual beings are made in the image of God, we can only infer from Scripture. Of the many attributes Christians often cite as distinctions between mankind and animals as evidence man is made in the image of God, these same attributes are found in heavenly beings.

Put simply, in our fallen state we may never fully grasp what encompasses being made "in the image of God." God is infinite, and simply trying to comprehend God's attributes can sometimes seem overwhelming.

But on the flip side, should it be a surprise that spiritual beings have attributes of their Creator who is Spirit as well? We can be sure of what God's Word teaches: humans are made in the image of God and are distinct from animals by having a spiritual aspect. I'm not aware of any major theological problems if one considers spiritual beings as being made in the image of God. Therefore, it may be wise to leave open the possibility that heavenly beings are made in the image of God.

29. Did the serpent tempt Eve while in the tree of the knowledge of good and evil?

Christians generally use illustrations of the Garden of Eden that place the serpent in a tree — usually the tree of the knowledge of good and evil. In fact, we do so at the Creation Museum in Petersburg, Kentucky:

Is there any justification for such a view?

What Does Scripture Say?

Nowhere in the Scriptures do we read that the serpent was in the tree — any tree. In fact, the opposite may well be deduced, as the serpent was compared to the *beasts of the field* twice:

> Now the serpent was more cunning than any beast *of the field* which the LORD God had made. And he said to the woman, "Has God indeed said, 'You shall not eat of every tree of the garden'?" (Genesis 3:1, emphasis mine).

> So the LORD God said to the serpent: "Because you have done this, you are cursed more than all cattle, and more than *every beast of the field*; on your belly you shall go, and you shall eat dust all the days of your life" (Genesis 3:14, emphasis mine).

If the Bible compares the serpent with beasts of the field, then it may well have been one. For the most part, beasts of the field are simply that: beasts found in the field. However, we must leave open the possibility that some of the beasts of the field could have climbed trees. After all, we cannot be sure of all the animals that fall into this category. So this alone doesn't necessarily rule out the serpent being in the tree when it deceived Eve.

If we look closer at the initial stages of the deception by the serpent, we find:

Now the serpent was more cunning than any beast of the field which the Lord God had made. And he said to the woman, "Has God indeed said, 'You shall not eat of every tree of the garden'?" And the woman said to the serpent, "We may eat the fruit of the trees of the garden; but of the fruit of the tree which is in the midst of the garden, God has said, 'You shall not eat it, nor shall you touch it, lest you die' " (Genesis 3:1–3).

Pay close attention to what Eve said here. She refers to the tree in the *midst* of the garden (which is where both the tree of life and tree of the knowledge of good and evil are – Genesis 2:9). Why would she say it like this if she were referring to a tree that the serpent is sitting in? If the serpent were really in the tree, then it makes more sense that she would respond something like: "We may eat the fruit of the trees of the garden;

Figure 16. The serpent in the tree of the knowledge of good and evil as depicted at the Creation Museum

but of the fruit of the tree *which you are sitting in*, God has said, 'You shall not eat it, nor shall you touch it, lest you die.' "

Of course, the Scriptures do not reveal the exact location of their discussion, but instead point to a tree elsewhere *in the midst* of the Garden — perhaps not too far off.

Now, this may be a strong argument against the serpent being in the tree; however, we still cannot completely rule out the possibility. If some insist that the serpent had to be in the tree, then they can certainly put forward an argument. On the other hand, most images of the serpent tempting Eve from the tree are likely for dramatic impact. It's just good to keep what Scripture teaches in mind.

30. Was there pain before the Fall?

To the woman He said: "I will greatly multiply your sorrow and your conception; in pain you shall bring forth children; your desire shall be for your husband, and he shall rule over you" (Genesis 3:16).

During the Fall, these words of Scripture ring out. Since the world was originally very good (Genesis 1:31) and truly perfect (Deuteronomy 32:4) — without any death or suffering of living creatures (Genesis 1:29–30) — would pain have existed before the Fall?

Let's examine what the Bible tells us. When Adam and Eve sinned against God, the world went from a *perfect* state to an *imperfect* state. The Lord cursed the ground (Genesis 3:17) and animals (Genesis 3:14) and sentenced mankind to die (Genesis 2:17, 3:18).

"Increased Pain"

From a cursory glance at Genesis 3:16, one may think that pain was part of this original perfectly created world. Let's take a look at this verse where the Lord is speaking to Eve and judging her due to her sin of eating from the tree of the knowledge of good and evil:

To the woman He said, "I will greatly multiply your pain [Hebrew: *itstsabown*] in childbirth, in pain [Hebrew: *etseb*] you will bring forth children; yet your desire will be for your husband, and he will rule over you" (NASB).

Some may assume that if pain was to be multiplied, then there was already pain — the intensity merely increased.[72] But is this correct? To understand this passage better, let's look at the Hebrew words used for pain and dive deeper into the Scriptures. The Hebrew words used for *pain* in Genesis 3:16 are *itstsabown* and *etseb*.

What Kind of Pain Increased?

Both words have similar definitions, meaning "pain" and "sorrows," with other connotations like "hurt" or "labor." So their differences are miniscule. But really there is a two-fold aspect to this pain. There is physical pain in the actual birthing process (most mothers can attest to this) and mental anguish (e.g., sorrows) associated with having children in a sin-cursed world.

Consider that Eve not only went through the pain of child bearing during delivery, but she also had to endure the loss of Abel, her own son, slain by his own brother. Consider also Mary, who saw her son Jesus die on the Cross. So there are two prongs to this, and, of course, seeing one of your children die is an extreme example. But it would be rare, if not impossible, to find a mother who has not seen her children suffer in some manner, from starvation to sickness, cuts, scrapes, and so on.

Does "Increased Pain" Mean Pain Before the Fall

Let's evaluate these two types of pain with regard to pre-Fall times. When dealing with mental anguish, such is brought on by the suffering or death of a child. But in a pre-Fall world with no death or its associated aspect of suffering (Romans 5:12), this pain would have been nonexistent. So an increase (where death and suffering entered the creation) wouldn't necessarily mean that this pain previously existed, but its mere entrance into the world made for an increase. From nothing to something is obviously an increase.

With regard to physical pain, as in childbearing, a similar reading can be applied. Increased pain doesn't necessarily mean pain before.

Consider what physical pain is. With your hand, you can touch a surface that is warm and you can detect the warm surface. There is no pain involved, merely sensation. However, if the surface temperature increases, at some point the sensation turns to pain.

In the same way, if I were to put my hand between two objects that merely rested against my hand, then I would have sensation. But if the objects began to "sandwich" my hand and continued to squeeze together, there would become a point where it is no longer mere sensation but pain.

Increased physical pain doesn't mean there was pain before, but merely *sensations that were useful.* So pain wasn't a part of the original creation, but sensation — the sense of touch — was.

What Happened at the Fall That Allowed Us to Feel Pain?

This brings up another point: what changed during the Fall to result in pain? There are actually several possibilities, such as:

1. Sensation, as a whole, intensified at the Fall to permit pain.
2. Innerworkings of the body (e.g., the pelvis bones for childbearing) no longer function as originally designed, causing increased sensation.
3. Potential design changes at the Fall (e.g., pelvic bones for child-bearing) resulted in increased sensation.
4. God no longer upholds the world in a perfect state so that extreme sensation can now be felt resulting in pain. Recall that while the Israelites wandered in the desert for 40 years, their clothes did not wear out and their feet didn't swell (Deuteronomy 8:4; Nehemiah 9:21). Remember that Shadrach, Meshach, and Abednego were in the fiery furnace where no flame affected them (Daniel 3:27). Moses died at 120 years old, and yet his eyes were not dim and his natural vigor was not diminished (Deuteronomy 34:7). With God upholding everything in a perfect state, there would have been no pain.

In fact, pain may be a combination of these or other factors in a post-Fall world.

Does Genesis 3:16 Reference Pain before the Fall?

When Adam and Eve sinned against God by eating of the fruit of the tree of knowledge of good and evil, there was a change. Genesis 3:7 points out that after they ate, they felt *ashamed* and realized they were naked. So, really, they had a sense of pain or hurting from this moment — which Scripture lists as *shame* (cf. Genesis 3:7 in contrast to Genesis 2:25) as well as *fear* (Genesis 3:10).

So when the Lord spoke to the woman and said that she would have increased pain and sorrows in childbearing, this is not to be taken as compared to the pre-Fall point, but from the Fall to the point when the Lord spoke. She began feeling pain due to sin, but then the Lord revealed there was much more to come (greatly increase the pains). And, of course, it finally results in death (Genesis 3:19).

The Lord pointed out that if she thought this pain they were feeling at that point was bad, she hadn't felt anything yet! In light of this, it may not be wise to use Genesis 3:16, which was discussing pain in a situation post-Fall, as a reflection of a pre-Fall world.

Something to Look Forward To

Regardless, sin led to pain as well as death and suffering. But this is not the final chapter. Heaven will be like the pre-Fall world, and there will be no more death or suffering or pain. It gives Christians something to look forward to.

> And God will wipe away every tear from their eyes; there shall be no more death, nor sorrow, nor crying. There shall be no more pain, for the former things have passed away (Revelation 21:4).

31. Was the fruit an apple? How did Eve know it was edible?

If you were to open a children's book about Adam and Eve and read about their sin, chances are that it would say Adam and Eve ate an "apple." Having children of my own and receiving kind gifts relating to Genesis, such as Bibles for kids, I usually have to look them over for any red flags. When these children's books say that the fruit was an "apple," I usually get frustrated — so, I get frustrated a lot, as this is a common problem (like the righteous anger Nehemiah felt in Nehemiah 5:1–7)!

It's not just in children's books. For example, this idea made its way into the encyclopedia:

> Many people believe an apple was the fruit that, according to the Bible, Adam and Eve ate in the Garden of Eden.[73]

The confusion of this fruit with the apple may be due to the similarity of the two words in the Latin translation of the Bible, known as the Vulgate. The word *evil* in the tree's name in Latin is *mali* (Genesis 2:17). The word *apple* in other places is *mala* (Proverbs 25:11) or *malum* (Song of Solomon 2:3). It seems like this similarity may have led to the confusion. In the original Hebrew, the words are not even close. The word in Genesis 2:17 for *evil* is *rah*, while the word for *apples* in Proverbs 25:11 and Song of Solomon 2:3 is *tappuwach*.

Why not an Apple?

Simply put, the Bible doesn't say the fruit was an apple. Furthermore, while apples are mentioned in Scripture (e.g., Song of Solomon 2:3, 8:5; Joel 1:12), they are not mentioned in the Garden of Eden, which is where the tree of the knowledge of good and evil was located. The forbidden fruit was indeed a *real* fruit, but not necessarily an apple. It was the fruit that came from the tree of the knowledge of good and evil.

Figure 17. Fruit as shown in the Creation Museum

Figure 18. Fruit as shown on the cover of *Answers* magazine, July–August 2009 (which was modeled after several fruits)

Figure 19. Fruit as shown in *A Is for Adam* (one of the best children's books on Genesis)[74]

God told Adam and Eve they could eat of every tree's fruit that had seed in it (Genesis 1:27–29), and apples have seeds in them. This may be a clue that the fruit of the tree of the knowledge of good and evil did not have seed in it.

The Fruit

What did fruit from the tree of the knowledge of good and evil look like? We simply don't know. However, there are speculations. In fact, various artists have developed different depictions.

This last one, which was done for children, could be used for humor as well. After illustrator Dan Lietha deliberately designed the fruit to not look like an apple, leading apologist Ken Ham has joked that this fruit looks rather similar to a hand grenade! This joke, which is now used by others as well, can be used as example of the truly devastating implications if eaten!

Regardless, we simply have no idea what the fruit looked like and only speculation within biblical limits is warranted.

How did Eve know the fruit was edible and desirable to make one wise?

Some have wondered how Eve knew that the fruit was edible and, for that matter, desirable to make one wise. Let's address this first part first.

> And the LORD God commanded the man, saying, "Of every tree of the garden you may freely eat; but of the tree of the knowledge of good and evil you shall not eat, for in the day that you eat of it you shall surely die" (Genesis 2:16–17).

Here, Adam was commanded not to eat, and this command made it to Eve as well; albeit, she did not articulate it properly to the serpent (Genesis 3:2–3). Therefore, one may assume that the fruit would be impossible to eat (inedible).

However, take note of what the Lord God says: "for in the day you eat of it." The Lord knew that Adam would eat. So the fruit was edible.[75] However, I do not suggest that this was the reason Eve knew the fruit to be edible. The Bible reveals something else:

> So when the woman saw that the tree was good for food, that it was pleasant to the eyes, and a tree desirable to make one wise, she took of its fruit and ate. She also gave to her husband with her, and he ate (Genesis 3:6).

Eve noticed something in Genesis 3:6. It says that she saw that the fruit was good for food. So she was not reminiscing about what God had said, but something else had caught her eye regarding the fruit.

Keep in mind that mankind was not permitted to eat the fruit of the tree of the knowledge of good and evil, but God did not give any warning to animals. It is possible that an animal, perhaps even the serpent, took some of the fruit and ate before Eve so that she could see that this fruit was good for food.

Second, seeing the fruit being eaten may have been a triggering action for Eve to realize that the fruit could be eaten by them as well. This very thought process in turn could be what made her think she had gained wisdom (e.g., if an animal could eat it, then so could she and Adam). Wisdom involves acquiring knowledge (see Proverbs 8:12). Note that Eve didn't have to eat to gain wisdom — or what she interpreted to be wisdom. The aspect of gaining wisdom was not based on eating the fruit, but on visual acuity. However, I would not be too strict on this, as there could be something else to this.

Of course, there may have been a bit more deception than this. Had the serpent eaten in front of her, he could have cleverly made it appear as though he had gained some wisdom. Regardless, she most likely saw something eat that fruit in order for her to solidify that it was edible and desirable for gaining wisdom. It was, after all, a fruit, and fruit is edible. Due to God's command not to eat, she would have known it was off limits and should have realized from that command that it was able to be eaten. Something she saw was the final trigger for her to:

1. Realize the fruit was indeed edible
2. See that it was pleasing to the eye
3. Desire it for gaining wisdom

Conclusion

Either way, Eve's actions and thought processes mimicked that of James 1:14–15. She cannot blame the serpent entirely for its cunning deception, but it was her own actions of eating that cannot be ignored — and the same with Adam (2 Corinthians 11:3). So we should learn that we too should not be deceived, which is why checking things against Scripture and viewing the Scriptures as the authority should be the goal of any Christian (Acts 17:11).

32. Why were Eve's eyes not opened until Adam ate?

This also answers the related question: why did they feel the need to wear clothes?

The account of Adam and Eve eating the fruit in Scripture states:

> So when the woman saw that the tree was good for food, that it was pleasant to the eyes, and a tree desirable to make one wise, she took of its fruit and ate. She also gave to her husband with her, and he ate. Then the eyes of both of them were opened, and they knew that they were naked; and they sewed fig leaves together and made themselves coverings (Genesis 3:6–7).

There are a host of possibilities why Eve's eyes were not opened until Adam ate. The obvious ones are:

1. They ate so close to the same time that the time difference was negligible.
2. The effects were not immediate, but took a short amount of time (perhaps a matter of seconds or minutes) for them to feel the shame and for their eyes to be opened.

Other answers have some potential as well. Consider:

3. The original command not to eat was given to Adam, so there may have been no bearing on Eve when she ate. In other words, just because she ate, it was meaningless. (However, I would lean against this view since Eve pointed out to the serpent in Genesis 3:2 that God's command encompassed her as well.)
4. Adam was responsible for his wife. In fact, the woman was created for the man (1 Corinthians 11:9), and so the created order began

with Adam (which Satan, through the serpent, refused to acknowledge when he approached Eve first). So Adam would have had to fall for their eyes to be opened. Simply put, Adam was the one responsible, *even* for his wife's actions.

5. Both had dominion, so both Adam and Eve had to fall for the change to occur. This perspective is based on Genesis 1:26–28, where Adam and Eve were given dominion together. In other words, for the entire dominion of man to fall, both had to sin.

Think of it conversely. If Adam had eaten first, would the same thing have happened? In the shared-dominion perspective, the answer would be yes. If Adam had eaten first, nothing would have appeared to happen, but when Eve would have eaten, *then* *both* had sinned and the entire dominion would fall.

With this view, if Eve had eaten and Adam had not, then the dominion would *not* have fallen, and only Eve would have been punished and died. Of course, there are really no "what ifs," so we shouldn't get caught up in too much of this type of thinking. Notice that the repercussion of Eve's sin affected *her* and subsequently all women since that original sin (Genesis 3:16). But notice Adam's punishment in Genesis 3:17–19 — the ground was cursed (i.e., the whole of the dominion). The Apostle Paul revealed the extent of this curse in Romans 8:20–22 as being the whole of creation, which is why we need a new heavens and a new earth.

In fact, this view could be coupled with the previous view (number 4). Both Adam and Eve had dominion, but Adam was ultimately the responsible party. Consider Romans 5:12 in regard to these last two viewpoints:

> Therefore, just as through one man sin entered the world, and death through sin, and thus death spread to all men, because all sinned (Romans 5:12).

Naturally, these last two views (4 and 5) may be reading too much into the account, but it is worth considering in light of Scripture. After all, Adam received the blame for sin's entrance, so he was the responsible party. However, the answer may simply be that Adam and Eve ate at practically the same time, or the effect may have had a slight delay (seconds to minutes). But when looking closely at this passage, one can't help but discuss what exactly Scripture means by, "their eyes were opened" — let's evaluate this in the next section.

Why Did They Feel the Need to Wear Clothes?

Here are a couple of passages in regard to Adam and Eve having their eyes opened and realizing their nakedness:

> And they were both naked, the man and his wife, and were not ashamed (Genesis 2:25).

> Then the eyes of both of them were opened, and they knew that they were naked; and they sewed fig leaves together and made themselves coverings (Genesis 3:7).

When Adam and Eve sinned, the Bible says their eyes were opened. The very next statement says they realized they were naked — and then further, they decided to make clothes.

So their sin affected the way Adam and Eve *perceived* things (i.e., their eyes were opened). In fact, the shame they now felt was due to sinful nature, because they no longer perceived things in a perfect fashion. Hence, they viewed that their nakedness should be covered.

Note that nakedness was *not* a sin, but a fallen perception of nakedness and the associated shame was included in the sorrows and mental anguish they now felt. Even today, nakedness is bonded with shame, as people the world over wear clothes. In fact, this doctrine of clothing that comes out of a literal rendering of Genesis reveals that, by wearing clothes, cultures and religions all over the world are confirming the Bible's account is true.

For example, an atheistic worldview holds that people evolved from animals and *are* animals, so why wear clothes? Some would say that we need clothes to stay warm, but some climates do not require any clothing for that purpose. Animals don't put on clothes. Consider other religions like Hinduism, where nothing is ultimately reality. Why wear clothes? (Islam borrows from the Bible, etc.) Please do not get me wrong, I am not asking people from these other religions to stop wearing clothes because it is a Judeo-Christian doctrine. In fact, we appreciate that they adhere to this doctrine.

What we would ask is that these people who have been taught their respective religions consider the *meaning* of wearing clothes and how that goes back biblically to our mutual ancestors, Adam and Eve, and sin. Such things show the validity of God's Word, pointing toward Christ who conquered sin on our behalf and now offers the free gift of salvation to all who believe.

33. Connections between Genesis and the Gospel

The Bible is the Word of God and reveals to us Jesus Christ, the Son of God, whether directly or indirectly. For example, Jesus even said, "For if you believed Moses, you would believe Me; for he wrote about Me" (John 5:46). The Fall of mankind, the entrance of sin, and the need for Christ to die for us originated in Genesis 3. Would we expect to see Christ there? Absolutely — but perhaps more than you realize.

Genesis 3 reveals the account of Eve being deceived by the serpent followed by Adam and Eve's sin of eating the fruit of the tree of the knowledge of good and evil. Genesis 3 also reveals the curses and repercussions of sin. Perhaps you are wondering where Christ is in this passage. Let's take a closer look.

Genesis 3:8–24: The Lord

The first reference to Christ is well known. It is called a "theophany" or, more precisely, a "Christophany." These are appearances of the Lord Jesus Christ in the Old Testament prior to Christ coming in the flesh (e.g., remember the Lord appearing to Abraham in Genesis 18; also see John 8:58). Keeping in mind who Christ is (the Creator God — John 1; Colossians 1; Hebrews 1), we need to remember that Jesus did not merely show up on the scene 2,000 years ago. He is the Creator, "the Word made flesh" as John puts it in John 1.

When the Lord was walking in the Garden of Eden after Adam and Eve sinned, He came to seek those who had been lost. This loving act is one of God's characteristics that shows that when man sinned, He still loved us and had a plan in place for salvation. When Christ stepped into history, it was to seek and save the lost (Luke 19:10).

In fact, this ties in with one common misconception. We often read or hear someone saying that Adam walked with God in the Garden of

Eden. However, this is not what the Bible says. When we read that the Lord was walking in the Garden, it was specifically *after* Adam and Eve sinned. In fact, the Lord came seeking them. This was in the cool of the day, so it was not the warmer portion of the day, but perhaps closer to evening or morning.[76]

Regardless, it may not be wise to say that Adam walked with God. Instead, due to sin, the Lord God came to seek and save mankind right from the start. And this was culminated in Christ's actions on the Cross.

Genesis 3:5: Knowing Good and Evil

Not everything the serpent said in Genesis 3 was a lie. This is common among deceivers: they sprinkle truth with lies. One thing the serpent said to Eve was that she would be *like* God, knowing good and evil.

Was this a "prophecy come true" for Satan (the influencer behind the serpent)? After all, in Genesis 3:22, God reveals that man had become like God, knowing good and evil. By no means is this a fulfilled prophecy of Satan, but common knowledge to him. As Satan had sinned in heavenly realms, God then experienced (i.e., knew intimately) a distinction between good and evil (evil is basically the absence of good).

When Adam and Eve sinned, they (and we) were subject to the same thing: an experiential knowledge of distinction between good and evil. So, in that sense, they had become *like* God. This is to be distinguished from being or becoming God.

But notice this connection to the gospel — mankind had become like God when we sinned. And the direct result was that God would become like man. In fact, He did become a Man — Jesus Christ — to die in our place.

Sin Connection: First Adam — Last Adam

When a perfect man, Adam, sinned in a perfect world, the whole world fell, including the dominion of Adam (think of it like this: if a king makes bad decisions, it affects his whole kingdom).

Christ, who became a man, was called the second or last Adam (1 Corinthians 15:45). If Adam is one type, Christ is another type.[77] Christ, unlike Adam, came into an imperfect world and yet lived a perfect and sinless life; Paul contrasts this in the following passages:

> And so it is written, "The first man Adam became a living being." The last Adam became a life-giving spirit (1 Corinthians 15:45).

> Therefore, just as through one man sin entered the world, and death through sin, and thus death spread to all men, because all sinned — (For until the law sin was in the world, but sin is not imputed when there is no law. Nevertheless death reigned from Adam to Moses, even over those who had not sinned according to the likeness of the transgression of Adam, who is a type of Him who was to come. But the free gift is not like the offense. For if by the one man's offense many died, much more the grace of God and the gift by the grace of the one Man, Jesus Christ, abounded to many (Romans 5:12–15).

In other words, all those who came from Adam die because we all sinned in Adam (Hebrews 7:9–10), and we all still sin. Since all of mankind come from Adam, we are all subject to this same death, which is the punishment for sin.

The fascinating thing is that not all will die in such a way because of Christ and His work on the Cross. Those in Christ will be made alive (John 5:24), and death will have no sting (1 Corinthians 15:55).

Genesis 3:11: Nakedness

In a perfect world, Adam and Eve were naked and felt no shame (Genesis 2:25); after sin, shame for nakedness had entered (Genesis 3:11). It affected Adam and Eve so much that they made fig leaf clothing and even hid from the Lord. Notice they hid from the Lord due to their nakedness even after they had made clothing! So sin's effect on nakedness was something serious, and most people still adhere to the doctrine of clothing today.

But why is nakedness brought out and discussed in so much detail here? Perhaps there is another connection to what Jesus went through on the Cross. John 19:23–24 reveals that Christ's own garments were taken from Him to reveal Him naked on the Cross, fulfilling Psalm 22:18.

Would Christ have been ashamed of being naked? Since He was not a sinner — and there is a relationship between sin and shame regarding nakedness in Genesis 3 (see also Revelation 3:18) — then it makes no sense that Christ would have been shamed by this. However, without a doubt, this was only one of many subtle attacks on Christ that could be classed as open shame from an outside, human perspective (consider Hebrews 6:6).

Genesis 3:15: Seed of a Woman/Virgin Birth

When Adam and Eve sinned against God, God cursed the ground, cursed the animals, and sentenced man to die. The world went from a perfect state to an imperfect state (which is why we need a new heavens and a new earth, by the way). But in the middle of all this, there is a beautiful promise — Genesis 3:15 mentions the seed of a woman, which Isaiah further speaks about when he says:

> Therefore the Lord Himself will give you a sign: Behold, the virgin shall conceive and bear a Son, and shall call His name Immanuel (Isaiah 7:14).

Genesis 3:15 is the first prophecy of Jesus being the seed of a woman or a virginal conception/fertilization that culminated in a virgin birth. Luke 1:26–35 explains this in much more detail — the miraculous entrance by our Savior into the world. As theologian Tim Chaffey eloquently explains in his book *God and Cancer*:

Many readers are familiar with the Christmas story. However, it is at the other end of Christ's earthly life that we see the fulfillment of the other promise made in Genesis 3:15. More than three decades later, Jesus was hanging on a cross outside of Jerusalem with nails piercing His wrists and one spike nailed through his feet. Of course, readers are probably familiar with the crucifixion of Jesus. However, many are not aware of the manner in which God's promise back in the Garden would be literally fulfilled. As a crucifixion victim, Christ would have literally bruised one of His heels. This is a natural result of crucifixion. As the crucifixion victim fights for air, he is forced to push himself upward so that he can take in a full breath. To do this, he must push his weight upward with his legs. However, because of the position in which the spike is driven through both feet, one of the victim's heels is pushed hard into the upright beam of the cross. As the victim repeatedly clamors for air, his heel is literally bruised against the cross. While this is extremely interesting and provides evidence for the supernatural origin of the Bible, it is not the most important part of the promise found in Genesis 3:15.

After Jesus died on the cross He was laid in a tomb. Three days later, He rose from the dead and began to appear to His followers. In the process of conquering death, the Creator also conquered the serpent. The Resurrection demonstrated Christ's power over the grave and guaranteed Satan's doom.[78]

Genesis 3:16: Increased Pain

In a sin-cursed and broken world, there are many aspects that the Lord could comment on. When speaking to Eve in Genesis 3, it is fascinating that the Lord says that she will have increased pain in childbearing.

The Hebrew word for *pain* is *etseb*, which strongly connotes "sorrow." Many quickly assume this means that women have to endure horrendous childbirth, which is no doubt one aspect. But consider the sorrow aspect. Eve saw one son murdered by another son (Cain killed Abel).

What mother would not go though a terrible delivery rather than see one of her children murdered? But Eve was not the only one to suffer such sorrow: Mary saw Jesus die on the Cross.

Genesis 3:18: Thorns

Cursed is the ground, but why mention thorns? Perhaps it is due to Christ knowing that one day a crown of thorns would be thrust upon His head (John 19:2–5).

Genesis 3:19: Return to Dust

Man was created from dust, and God breathed life into him (Genesis 2:7). When Adam and Eve sinned, they were, in essence, saying that they wanted a life without God. And so they were kicked out of the Garden of Eden into the very dust that was used to create Adam (Genesis 3:23).

God specifically planted a Garden and presented it perfectly to Adam (Genesis 2:8, 15). Now Adam was forced to plant his own garden (Genesis 3:23) and tend it in toil and by the sweat of his brow (Genesis 3:17–19).

And so it is with dust: we come from it, and we return to it. But Jesus Christ, being the Son of God when crucified and laid in a grave, did *not* return to dust. He rose again proving that He has power over life and death. In fact, Christ's body did not even see decay (Acts 13:35–37), fulfilling what was said in Psalm 16:10.

Genesis 3:21: Sacrifice

When Adam and Eve sinned, they were ashamed, knowing they were naked, and made fig leaf coverings for themselves. But the punishment for sin was death (Genesis 2:17), and the Lord God sacrificed animals to cover Adam and Eve's sin in Genesis 3:21 (garments/coats of skin). This very sacrifice was used to cover their nakedness from sin.

It set the stage for sacrifice with Abel offering fat portions, Noah offering sacrifices of clean animals, and Abraham and the Israelites offering sacrifices, which all pointed toward Christ, our Passover Lamb (1 Corinthians 5:7). For Christ is the ultimate and perfect sacrifice — the only one who could take the infinite punishment from an infinite God. This first sacrifice in *Genesis 3* was a model of what was to come — leading to Christ on the Cross.

Genesis 3:22: Eternal Life

The tree of life, once Adam and Eve sinned, could have theoretically given Adam and Eve eternal life in a sin-cursed world. And such was not the plan. This would actually be a terrible punishment for those who repent of their sins and turn to God. Can you imagine living forever in a sin-cursed world with no hope of something better? Thankfully, for those who love God and want to be with Him, God had another plan in place.

Jesus stepped in died for us and offers the free gift of salvation to all who receive. Consider the following passages:

For God so loved the world that He gave His only begotten Son, that whoever believes in Him should not perish but have everlasting life. For God did not send His Son into the world to condemn the world, but that the world through Him might be saved. He who believes in Him is not condemned; but he who does not believe is condemned already, because he has not believed in the name of the only begotten Son of God (John 3:16–18).

For He whom God has sent speaks the words of God, for God does not give the Spirit by measure. The Father loves the Son, and has given all things into His hand. He who believes in the Son has everlasting life; and he who does not believe the Son shall not see life, but the wrath of God abides on him (John 3:34–36).

Nor is there salvation in any other, for there is no other name under heaven given among men by which we must be saved (Acts 4:12).

And Jesus came and spoke to them, saying, "All authority has been given to Me in heaven and on earth. Go therefore and make disciples of all the nations, baptizing them in the name of the Father and of the Son and of the Holy Spirit, teaching them to observe all things that I have commanded you; and lo, I am with you always, even to the end of the age." Amen (Matthew 28:18–20).

Jesus Christ is the central figure in the Bible, so we should focus on Him, rather than Satan, the serpent, or even angels and heroes of the faith. God has been so gracious as to present the Bible to man. Let us not neglect it — but use it in every area of our lives.

34. What does it mean to be saved (and how does it relate to the Curse)?

A re you like me? I get tired of sitting down in the middle of something like a story, show, etc., and wondering what's going on. I think most people feel like this when they hear about Jesus for the first time. In my past, I would hear things like: "Good news! Good news! Here's how to get saved: Believe in Jesus!"

I was thinking, *Saved from what? Jesus who?* Obviously, there was something missing in the approach that these well-meaning Christians used with me, and it is important, then, to learn to be better witnesses.

Perfect Creation . . . Then the Bad News

First of all, it's tough to understand the good news of being saved if you don't understand the bad news. So let's go back to the beginning. In the beginning, God created everything:

> In the beginning God created the heavens and the earth (Genesis 1:1).[79]

When God created everything He said it was "very good." This meant that everything was perfect. The whole creation was perfect. In fact, God says that all His works are perfect, and we would expect that from a perfect God. Man lived in the perfectly created earth (i.e., a paradise) with a perfect relationship with God.

> Then God saw everything that He had made, and indeed it was very good. So the evening and the morning were the sixth day (Genesis 1:31).

> He is the Rock, His work is perfect; for all His ways are justice, a God of truth and without injustice; righteous and upright is He (Deuteronomy 32:4)

Because the original creation was perfect, there was no death before this (Genesis 1:29–30).[80] God gave man and woman the freedom of contrary choice.[81] The first two people God created were Adam and Eve, who were allowed to freely eat from any tree in the Garden of Eden except the tree of the knowledge of good and evil. They were to live forever with God. Again, there was no death. However, Eve was tempted by a serpent (being influenced by Satan, who had rebelled against God in the heavenly realm), and then both Adam and Eve also rebelled against God by eating from the tree of the knowledge of good and evil; thus, they sinned (sin is rebellion against God[82]).

> And the LORD God commanded the man, saying, "Of every tree of the garden you may freely eat; "but of the tree of the knowledge of good and evil you shall not eat, for in the day that you eat of it you shall surely die" (Genesis 2:16–17).

> Now the serpent was more cunning than any beast of the field which the LORD God had made. And he said to the woman, "Has God indeed said, 'You shall not eat of every tree of the garden'?" And the woman said to the serpent, "We may eat the fruit of the trees of the garden; "but of the fruit of the tree which is in the midst of the garden, God has said, 'You shall not eat it, nor shall you touch it, lest you die.'" Then the serpent said to the woman, "You will not surely die." For God knows that in the day you eat of it your eyes will be opened, and you will be like God, knowing good and evil."

> So when the woman saw that the tree was good for food, that it was pleasant to the eyes, and a tree desirable to make one wise, she took of its fruit and ate. She also gave to her husband with her, and he ate (Genesis 3:1–6).

The result of Adam's sin (rebellion against a Holy Creator) was God's judgment through many curses. God cursed the ground, which mankind had dominion over (Genesis 1:28), to bring forth thorns and thistles. He sentenced man and woman to die, fulfilling what was spoken in Genesis 2:17. He also cursed the animals and, especially, the serpent.

From this act of rebellion, we (i.e., humans, descendants of Adam) inherit "original sin." This, in a layman's sense, means that we are sentenced to die and are prone to sin because we were in Adam when he sinned.[83] In essence, these curses are like God removing some of His sustaining power, so the creation is no longer upheld in a perfect state, but in bondage to sin and death (Romans 8:21) — hence, we now suffer things like cancer, sickness, suffering, and finally, death.

> So the LORD God said to the serpent: "Because you have done this, you are cursed more than all cattle, and more than every beast of the field; on your belly you shall go, and you shall eat dust all the days of your life. And I will put enmity between you and the woman, and between your seed and her Seed; He shall bruise your head, and you shall bruise His heel."
>
> To the woman He said: "I will greatly multiply your sorrow and your conception; in pain you shall bring forth children; your desire shall be for your husband, and he shall rule over you."
>
> Then to Adam He said, "Because you have heeded the voice of your wife, and have eaten from the tree of which I commanded you, saying, 'You shall not eat of it': cursed is the ground for your sake; in toil you shall eat of it all the days of your life. Both thorns and thistles it shall bring forth for you, and you shall eat the herb of the field. In the sweat of your face you shall eat bread till you return to the ground, for out of it you were taken; for dust you are, and to dust you shall return" (Genesis 3:14–19).

> Therefore, just as through one man sin entered into the world, and death through sin, and thus death spread to all men, because all sinned (Romans 5:12).

In spite of our sin, God loved us so much that He had already planned a way for us to return to a perfect relationship with Him. To provide forgiveness and salvation, God gave the first prophecy of many regarding the way back to a restored relationship with Him. Genesis 3:15 says that the *seed* will be that of a woman.[84] This refers to the future event — the virgin birth of Jesus — being the "seed of a woman" and not of a man.

Death and Sacrifice Point Toward a Savior

In the New Testament, Paul confirms what is written in Genesis 2:17 when he says that the wages of sin is death. One sin is enough to cause death!

For the wages of sin is death (Romans 6:23).

Since the wages of sin is death, God, in Genesis 3, shows that a life must be taken to cover the sin of Adam and Eve. Therefore, to make a temporary atonement (cover the sins for a time), God killed these animals on behalf of Adam and Eve, clothing them with the skins.

For Adam and his wife the LORD God made tunics of skin, and clothed them (Genesis 3:21).

The punishment demanded from an infinitely holy God, who cannot look upon sin, is an infinite punishment. Animals are not infinite, and so, they cannot ultimately take away the sin, but merely cover it. Mankind needed a perfect, infinitely holy sacrifice. Jesus Christ, who is the infinite and holy Son of God, stepped into history to take that punishment on Himself. We ultimately need a perfect sacrifice, and the perfectly obedient life of Christ was God's plan for the ultimate atonement.

But after Adam and Eve sinned, people began making animal sacrifices to cover their sins — an animal life for sin. A few examples follow.

Abel

Abel also brought of the firstborn of his flock and of their fat. And the LORD respected Abel and his offering (Genesis 4:4).

Noah

Then Noah built an altar to the LORD, and took of every clean animal and of every clean bird, and offered burnt offerings on the altar (Genesis 8:20).

Abraham

Then Abraham lifted his eyes and looked, and there behind him was a ram caught in a thicket by its horns. So Abraham went and took the ram, and offered it up for a burnt offering instead of his son (Genesis 22:13).

Israelites

If the offering is a burnt offering from the herd, he is to offer a male without defect. He must present it at the entrance to the Tent of Meeting so that it will be acceptable to the LORD (Leviticus 1:3).

The Law of Moses (i.e., Genesis–Deuteronomy) revealed sin as rebellion against God. The moral laws are summarized in the Ten Commandments (Exodus 20; Deuteronomy 5). Even with the Law, people continued rebelling and turning away from God (Romans 3:20). But God sent the ultimate and final sacrifice — far greater than any animal sacrifice — that would be sufficient to cover sin against a perfect God (Hebrews 10:1–14).

Jesus Christ, the Savior, Steps into History

For God so loved the world that He gave His one and only begotten Son, that whoever believes in Him should not perish but have everlasting life (John 3:16).

God sent His Son (i.e., the second person of the triune God[85]), Jesus, to humble Himself and enter into a sin-cursed world to live a servant's life on earth just like one of us (Philippians 2:8). He entered the world just as was prophesied — through the virgin Mary. Jesus was without sin (1 John 3:5) and did everything perfectly according to the Law. Then He would allow mankind to sacrifice Him on the Cross. Jesus would be the final sacrifice because he obeyed God completely and was without defect — only He could satisfy the infinite punishment we deserve. His method of sacrifice (crucifixion) was even outlined many years before in Psalm 22. He was the perfect sacrifice (far exceeding the most perfect, unblemished animal) because He was the perfect man and also perfect God (Colossians 2:9).

> Do not think that I have come to abolish the Law or the Prophets; I have not come to abolish them but to fulfill them (Matthew 5:17; NIV).

When God stepped into His creation, He offered what is called "grace." Grace means that we were to be rightly punished for our wrongdoings, and then the one who sentenced us to that punishment took the punishment upon Himself because of love for us. We rightly deserved death by God's judgment. But God took that punishment upon Himself by dying in our place as Jesus Christ. He exercised that grace because of His love for us.

Jesus didn't come to the world to sentence it to death — the world was already condemned by sin. He came to save us from that sin. This indicates that God really is a God of love.

> For God did not send his Son into the world to condemn the world, but that the world through him might be saved (John 3:17).

> And you He made alive, who were dead in trespasses and sins, in which you once walked according to the course of this world, according to the prince of the power of the air, the spirit who now works in the sons of disobedience, among whom also we all once conducted ourselves in the lusts of our flesh, fulfilling the desires of the flesh and of the mind, and were by nature children of wrath, just as the others.
> But God, who is rich in mercy, because of His great love with which He loved us, even when we were dead in trespasses, made us alive together with Christ (by grace you have been saved), and raised us up together, and made us sit together in the heavenly

places in Christ Jesus, that in the ages to come He might show the exceeding riches of His grace in His kindness toward us in Christ Jesus (Ephesians 2:1–7).

A second death is still the punishment that God will give to those who do not turn to Him. The second death is called hell and is separation from God — being completely separated from all that is good.[86] Even Satan himself has no power there. Jesus came to be the final sacrifice to allow us to be saved from this penalty due to sin against a holy God.

When Jesus rose and conquered death, people no longer needed to present an animal sacrifice to cover up their sins. For those who trust in Christ will receive the gift of the Holy Spirit. The Bible warns that the only unforgivable sin is blasphemy against the Holy Spirit. All other sins can be forgiven up to the moment of death.

> Anyone who speaks a word against the Son of Man, it will be forgiven him; but whoever who speaks against the Holy Spirit, it will not be forgiven him, either in this age or in the age to come (Matthew 12:32).

Blasphemy against the Holy Spirit is rejecting the Holy Spirit to the point of death. The only way to reject the Holy Spirit is by not receiving Jesus as your Savior during your lifetime. This corresponds to Jesus saying that He was the only way back to God the Father.

> Jesus said to him, "I am the way, the truth, and the life. No one comes to the Father except through me" (John 14:6).

The Free Gift of Salvation: Belief in Christ

Jesus, being the perfect sacrifice, offers the free gift of salvation. God loves you so much that He sacrificed His own unblemished Son to suffer the wrath against sin and die on the Cross. He commands you to repent (change your mind and turn from sinful ways) and trust in Him:

> For godly sorrow produces repentance leading to salvation, not to be regretted; but the sorrow of the world produces death (2 Corinthians 7:10).[87]

The Bible is clear in several passages how to receive salvation. It doesn't mean you are perfect after you are saved, but it does mean that you are perfectly forgiven and saved from the penalty of sin by God's grace.

> For by grace you have been saved through faith, and that not of yourselves; it is the gift of God, not of works, lest anyone should boast (Ephesians 2:8–9).

> That if you confess with your mouth the Lord Jesus and believe in your heart that God has raised Him from the dead, you will be saved. For with the heart one believes unto righteousness, and with the mouth confession is made unto salvation (Romans 10:9–10).

> "He who believes and is baptized will be saved; but he who does not believe will be condemned (Mark 16:16).

> And he brought them out and said, "Sirs, what must I do to be saved?" So they said, "Believe on the Lord Jesus Christ, and you will be saved, you and your household" (Acts 16:30–31).

These verses point out the importance of belief in Jesus Christ. It is a simple and free gift. It doesn't matter how many steps you've taken away from God; it is only one step back. If you are not a Christian, then consider more deeply the claims of Jesus, and please take a few minutes to pray to God in the name of Jesus to forgive your sins and to receive Jesus Christ as the Lord of your life. Then please take some time to sit down with a Bible-believing pastor in a local church to help direct you as you begin your new life with Christ. Read your Bible every day and seek to understand and obey what you read.

35. Bonus Question: Who were the Nephilim (and the sons of God) in Genesis 6 and Numbers 13?

Now it came about, when men began to multiply on the face of the land, and daughters were born to them, that the sons of God [*bene Elohim*] saw that the daughters of men were beautiful; and they took wives for themselves, whomever they chose. Then the LORD said, "My Spirit shall not strive with man forever, because he also is flesh; nevertheless his days shall be one hundred and twenty years."

The **Nephilim** were on the earth in those days, and also afterward, when the sons of God [*bene Elohim*] came in to the daughters of men, and they bore *children* to them. Those were the mighty men who were of old, men of renown. Then the LORD saw that the wickedness of man was great on the earth, and that every intent of the thoughts of his heart was only evil continually (Genesis 6:1–5; NASB, emphasis added).

Then Caleb quieted the people before Moses and said, "We should by all means go up and take possession of it, for we will surely overcome it."

But the men who had gone up with him said, "We are not able to go up against the people, for they are too strong for us." So they gave out to the sons of Israel a bad report of the land which they had spied out, saying, "The land through which we have gone, in spying it out, is a land that devours its inhabitants; and all the people whom we saw in it are men of *great* size. There also we saw the **Nephilim** (the sons of Anak are part of the **Nephilim**); and we became like grasshoppers in our own sight, and so we were in their sight" (Numbers 13:30–33; NASB, emphasis added).

Genesis 6 and Numbers 13 (pre-Flood and post-Flood) use the term

Nephilim, and it has been the center of discussion for many years. At this point, the identity of the Nephilim and the sons of God is still being debated in Christian circles.[88] There is a popular unbiblical view that the Nephilim are space aliens. Of course, most Christians rightly reject this particular view for multiple reasons, but that is not for discussion in this chapter.

Four Major Views

Of the views with some biblical support, some believe that fallen angels fathered children with women, which resulted in giants called Nephilim. Some believe the sons of God were the result of fallen angels who overtook ungodly men to father children with women.

Others believe the term *sons of God* refers to the Sethites (descendants of Adam's son Seth). There are some minor views that are similar. Some use Psalm 82 to suggest that these sons of God were godly kings, rulers, or heads of leading family groups. This view has many similarities to the Sethite view, but sees the leaders/kings (as well as some other leaders of other tribes) as the godly ones. Because these views are similar, I will leave this minor view out and focus on the Sethite view, which should encompass the minor view for the most part.

Another variation of the Sethite view is that these godly men had relations with ungodly women, and the offspring followed after other gods — not the one, true God — and fell away in tremendous ways. We will call this view the "fallen men" view. There are other minor views as well as other minor non-biblical views but these four will be discussed here.

Nephilim — What Does It Mean?

There is a great deal of confusion over the word *Nephilim*. No one today really knows what it means. It is related to the verb series "to fall" (*naphal*) in Hebrew, which is why some direct this to fallen angels or more appropriately, the offspring thereof. However, this also gives strong support to the view that *men* had fallen away from God. These two concepts gave rise to the various views mentioned in table 6.

Table 6. Brief summary of the four popular Nephilim views discussed

Name	View in short
Fallen angels view	Satan and/or his fallen angels bred with human women and had offspring that were called Nephilim.
Fallen angels overtook men view	Fallen angels and/or Satan possessed men and caused them to breed with women, whose offspring were the Nephilim.
Sethite view	The sons of God were the godly line from Adam to Seth down to Noah, and the Nephilim were fallen children who sought after false gods.
Fallen men view	Godly men ("sons of God") took ungodly wives, and their descendants (Nephilim) followed after false gods, rejected God, and fell far from God in wickedness.

Many have associated the Nephilim with giants. Giant traits may not have been *limited* to Nephilim alone: Goliath, a giant, was not considered Nephilim. As mentioned, the term *Nephilim* is unclear in definition. It is related to the verb "to fall" and the King James Version translates it as *giants* from the influence of the Latin Vulgate's (early Latin translation by Jerome) term *gigantes* as well as the context from Numbers 13. The context of Genesis 6 does not reveal they were giants. There may have been some influence on the Latin Vulgate by the Septuagint's (Greek translation of the Old Testament about 200–300 years before Christ) use of the Greek word *gigentes*.

Fallen Angels View

- Sons of God = Fallen angels
- Nephilim = Mix of human and angel

This is one of the most popular views. Of course, being one of the more popular views, it also has invited considerable criticism. This view stems from angels being called "sons of God," or interpreted as such, in

Job 1:6, 2:1, 38:7. In fact, if the Nephilim were indeed half human/half fallen angel then it would give great understanding to the many ancient religious views after Babel, including demigods. As pointed out, the word *Nephilim* is related to the verb series "to fall" in Hebrew, giving support to the view that this is related to fallen angels. So it does hold some status among biblical scholars.

Marriage in Heaven

One early argument against this angelic view was that, according to Jesus, angels don't marry (Matthew 22:30). This has been responded to many times and it is rightly pointed out that this is referring to angels *in heaven*, not fallen angels on earth. So the option is left open that fallen angels may very well do this. But there are other more important issues at stake.

Peter and Jude

Defenders of this view also find support in two key New Testament passages: 2 Peter 2:1–11 and Jude 4–8.

> For if God did not spare the angels who sinned, but cast them down to hell and delivered them into chains of darkness, to be reserved for judgment; and did not spare the ancient world, but saved Noah, one of eight people, a preacher of righteousness, bringing in the flood on the world of the ungodly; and turning the cities of Sodom and Gomorrah into ashes, condemned them to destruction, making them an example to those who afterward would live ungodly . . . (2 Peter 2:4–6).

> For certain men have crept in unnoticed, who long ago were marked out for this condemnation, ungodly men, who turn the grace of our God into lewdness and deny the only Lord God and our Lord Jesus Christ. But I want to remind you, though you once knew this, that the Lord, having saved the people out of the land of Egypt, afterward destroyed those who did not believe. And the

angels who did not keep their proper domain, but left their own abode, He has reserved in everlasting chains under darkness for the judgment of the great day; as Sodom and Gomorrah, and the cities around them in a similar manner to these, having given themselves over to sexual immorality and gone after strange flesh, are set forth as an example, suffering the vengeance of eternal fire. Likewise also these dreamers defile the flesh, reject authority, and speak evil of dignitaries (Jude 4–8).

These verses do not specifically mention the Nephilim, nor do they clearly state that fallen angels had sexual relations with women. However, they do place "the angels who sinned" (2 Peter 2:4), "who did not keep their proper domain, but left their own abode" (Jude 6), in the same context as Noah. Both passages seem to compare the sin of these angels with the sin of the people of Sodom and Gomorrah who had "in a similar manner to these . . . given themselves over to sexual immorality and gone after strange flesh" (Jude 7). Genesis 19:5 reveals that the men of Sodom lusted after the two angels who had gone into Lot's house.

It is important to understand that while these verses seem to lend strong support to the fallen angel view, they do not make a watertight case for it. For example, expositor Dr. John Gill argues for the contrary with regard to Jude 6–7.[89] Jude 8 says that these sinners who crept into the church were doing the same things (defiling the flesh, rejecting authority, and speaking evil of dignitaries) as the three groups mentioned immediately before this in verses 5–7. So the context reveals that those in Sodom and Gomorrah defiled the flesh (Genesis 19:4–7), angels that sinned rejected authority (Isaiah 14:12–16; Revelation 12:3–4), and the Lord's people who miraculously came out of Egypt spoke evil of dignitaries (Number 14:26–35). To equate angels with defiling the flesh in light of this verse may not be wise.

The context in Jude is discussing ungodly people who have crept into the Church and a warning about their future. Such sin and unrighteousness is nothing new. God will destroy those who are ungodly and creep into the Church, just as He did the other ungodly people and angels mentioned. Their condemnation will be the same. This type of logical thinking applies to 2 Peter 2 as well — the angels sinning, the sin of those in Noah's day, the sin of Sodom and Gomorrah, etc., are not all the same, but sin nonetheless.

Angelic DNA

One of the prime arguments against this view is that angels are spiritual and don't have DNA to combine with a woman's DNA. Though this can be argued because angels did take on the appearance of men such as Gabriel (Daniel 9:21; Luke 1:11–20) and the two angels sent to destroy Sodom (Genesis 19:1–13), assuming these angels had reproductive capabilities is another issue. Also, these angels that appeared as men were not the fallen ones. We have no biblical support of fallen angels ever appearing as men or of having physical DNA.

The spiritual *can* produce physical offspring, as witnessed by the Holy Spirit overshadowing Mary. However, the Holy Spirit is the Creator and has that power (Psalm 104:30). Do fallen angels? The Bible simply doesn't reveal this.

Commentaries and Translations: Sons of God

While many commentaries, as well as the Codex Alexandrinus manuscript of the Septuagint, refer to the sons of God in *poetic* Job 1:6 and Job 2:1 as angels, this may not be the best argument for the *narrative history* in Genesis 6 for a couple of reasons. Some commentaries leave open the possibility that these could be referring to godly men and/or magistrates on earth, who were human.[90]

The author of Job was aware of the term used for angel (*Kalm mal'ak*), as Eliphaz the Temanite used it in Job 4:18. So if the sons of God were referring to angels, then why not say it? It may be too much to say for sure that these two verses early in Job are referring to angels, but even so, it wouldn't be referring to fallen ones. There are no other instances in

Scripture that refer to fallen angels or demons as sons of God to verify this in Job.

Sometimes we fall into the mistake of assuming one name or phrase in a portion of Scripture is the same thing/type as another portion of Scripture. Though this may be the case, one shouldn't be dogmatic about it. For example, the Hebrew word for *Babel* or *Babylon* is referring to two distinct empires. If we find *Babel* referring to Nebuchadnezzar, we shouldn't assume it is the Babel that followed soon after the Flood.

Regardless though, Job 38:7 is an excellent example of angels being called sons of God. However, this is referring to angels during the creation week, before any of them fell (which would have to be after God's declaration that everything was "very good" in Genesis 1:31). So this doesn't give much support to fallen angels being called sons of God.

Another argument in opposition to this view is that godly men were sometimes called son(s) of God, such as Adam in Luke 3:38. Other passages also confirm that Christians are called sons of God (Matthew 5:9; Romans 8:14, 19; Galatians 3:26).

Although each of these is in Greek and the "sons of God" for Genesis 6 is in Hebrew, they are both rendered correctly as "sons of God." Luke 6:35 renders the term "sons of the Most High." Also, Psalm 82:6 has "sons of the most high." Hosea 1:10 points out that people will also be called "sons of the living God" (note the added descriptor *living*) in Hebrew.

Again, this is not identical to the Hebrew in Genesis or Job, but still demonstrates that humans can be called sons of God in another format and another language. So we have instances where humans are called:

- Sons of God (5 times in Greek)
- Sons of the Most High (1 time in Greek; 1 time in Hebrew)
- Sons of the living God (1 time in Hebrew)

Why is "sons of God" in Hebrew suddenly off-limits to refer to humans when God has already used similar terms for calling godly men by such a godly title? It seems unlikely that God would put *fallen* angels in a class with *un-fallen* angels, Israelites (God's chosen people), and Christians (the Bride of Christ). I doubt that God would want confusion between fallen angels and His Bride! Some dismiss the verse in Hosea out of hand, but it shouldn't be neglected. Other verses point out that men can be children of God, such as Psalm 73:15 and Deuteronomy 32:5. Thus, God-fearing men can also rightly be called sons of God.

One response is that the reason Adam and Christians were called son(s) of God was because they were made directly by God in one fashion or another — Adam from the dust by God's hand and Christians are made new creations (2 Corinthians 5:17). Along with this then, angels, who were directly created by God during creation week, could also hold to this title.

However, there are other direct creations by God, such as the original sea creatures, land animals, and so on. Are these also sons of God? Few would say they are. Also, godly men of the Old Testament would one day be new creations in Christ and, by the foreknowledge of God, could easily have been called "sons of God." So this argument really doesn't make a case exclusively for the angelic view, but could also be used for godly men as well. To clarify, this is not to be confused with the only begotten Son of God, Jesus Christ, who was the unique and perfect (i.e., only begotten) Son of God.

Theological Problem: An Evil Report

Another theological problem presents itself for the fallen angels view when we take a closer look at the Anakites (descendants of Anak), descendants of the Nephilim according to Numbers 13:33. The Anakites were not completely wiped out by Joshua (Joshua 11:22). The Bible never records their line ending. Thus, there is no reason to assume the descendants of Anak are not still living today. In fact, they have probably interbred with many other people groups since then.

This theological problem has been challenged, though, and rightly so because Numbers 13:30–33 is part of a bad/evil report spread among the Israelites. But was the information false about the Anakites being

Nephilim? Was the report of the Anakites being Nephilim accurate or inaccurate, as even falsehoods often contain some aspects of truth?

For example, we know that Anakites were indeed in the land, as Joshua went to war with them later. So which aspects of this report were false and which were true? We get a clue when Caleb and Joshua answer the congregation who was grumbling about the bad report in Numbers 14:6–9. The following table breaks down the bad report and analyzes what was false and what was not challenged.

Table 7. Bad Report: Challenged or Not?

Bad report indicates	Was this challenged by Joshua and Caleb?
The land devours its inhabitants.	Challenged: The land was exceedingly good, flowing with milk and honey, according to Joshua and Caleb.
All the men were of great size; the spies seemed very small in their sight (like grasshoppers).	Challenged: Joshua and Caleb told them to not be afraid of the people of the land. They didn't comment on the size, but many may have been giants, since they do point out that people were afraid of them.
Anakites were there.	Not challenged
Nephilim were there.	Not challenged
Anakites were descendants of the Nephilim.	Not challenged
Anakites were only a part of the Nephilim.	Not challenged

So it may not be the best argument to say that the false report meant that the Anakites were not Nephilim; this point (and other aspects of the report mentioned above) was never addressed as being false. Thus, the argument stands that Nephilim were the descendants of Anak and were around post-Flood. This also reveals that Nephilim can exist without being offspring of "sons of God," as they are only listed as being descendants of Anak.

Recall that Moses, who penned Genesis, said in Genesis 6:4 that the Nephilim were on the earth pre-Flood and also afterward. Some translations say "and after that," and one could argue that this was still referring to a pre-Flood time. However, it makes much more sense that this phrase refers to this post-Flood event, especially since Genesis 6 was penned by Moses after the Flood.

Acts 17:26 indicates all nations are of "one blood" or "one man." If some nations are a combination of angelic blood and Adamic blood, as the Anakites would have been in this view, as well as the Nephilim pre-Flood, then there is a major problem — Acts 17:26 would be wrong. The Anakites were still living and breeding with many other people groups during Paul's time. Thus, it presents a problem to say angels bred with women.

Men of Renown . . . and Men in General

Another problem presents itself from the rest of Genesis 6:4 ". . . Those were the mighty men who were of old, men [*iysh*] of renown." In Genesis 6:4, the phrase "men of renown" uses the Hebrew word *iysh*. This term is used consistently as "man" or descendants of Adam — even Adam used it of himself in Genesis 2:23, yet it is never used of fallen angels, demons, or of Satan. It was used for some *unfallen* angels when they took the form of a man, though. If the Nephilim were crossbreeds between men and fallen angels, then why did the Bible use the term men (*iysh*) as opposed to something that would lead us to believe they were not fully men?

If we follow the context of *iysh* (man) into the following verses in Genesis 6, we find:

- Verse 4: Nephilim are *men* of renown
- Verse 5: wickedness of *man* was great
- Verse 6: God was sorry He made *man* on earth
- Verse 7: God would blot out *man* from earth
- Verse 8/9: Noah found favor with God and was a righteous *man*

The context reveals that Noah was compared with and amongst the *men* being discussed in Genesis 6, yet unlike them he was righteous (Genesis 6:9). There is no mention of Noah being fully human and other men being half-breeds, but merely that he was righteous among them. Presenting Noah as righteous among his generation lends support for the view that the sons of God were human.

Jesus and Spirits with Flesh and Bones

Perhaps the most devastating argument against this view came from Jesus Himself. We have no instance in Scripture where fallen angels ever materialized, as previously stated. This is significant because Christ offered proof of His Resurrection when the disciples questioned Him in Luke 24:37–43. In this context, Jesus said, "A spirit does not have flesh and bones as you see I have."

If fallen angels or demons, which are spirit, could materialize, then this calls into question the entire Resurrection of Christ. Christ says spirits do not have flesh and bones, so it would seem these entities can't make physical bodies for themselves.

In light of some of these criticisms, this popular view may not be the best one, though many great scholars hold to it and it should be at least respected. I encourage deeper study in both the view and the responses as I am only touching the surface in this chapter.

Fallen Angels Overtook Men View

- Sons of God = Men overtaken by fallen angels/demons
- Nephilim = 100 percent human

This view has some similarities to the previous view in that the sons of God have a relationship to fallen angels. The sons of God would be men who were overtaken (possessed) by fallen angels and/or demons.[91] Unlike the previous view, this one holds that the offspring were not a mix of human and angel, but completely human. Of course, some of the arguments against the sons of God being angels in the previous section apply here as well.

It is possible for men to be overcome by Satan or demons. Men can easily be overcome or influenced by Satan such as Judas in Luke 22:3. Demons have often entered into people, such as in Mark 5:15.

The question really is this: would such people who are overtaken by demons and/or fallen angels warrant the title "sons of God"? In the gospel accounts, many people were overtaken by demons, but never were they titled "sons of God." Other biblical passages do not mention people who were overcome by evil spirits or demons as "sons of God" either.

In this view, though, there is no problem with Nephilim appearing pre-Flood, getting wiped out, and then reappearing as this happened again. According to this view, the offspring/Nephilim are still 100 percent descendants of Adam and Eve, thus eligible to receive salvation if they placed their faith in the Lord Jesus Christ. The children would have been conceived in sin. But this is nothing new in light of original sin that affects us all since Adam sinned in the Garden.

One problem associated with this view is this: are Nephilim still being born today? If not, then why was it no longer mentioned in the Bible after Moses, especially with the many demon-possessed and satanic entrances into men surrounding the time of Christ? So, by this view, any of us could potentially be Nephilim!

Also, it would seem strange that offspring by this union would require an entirely different term (Nephilim) to describe them. Although this may not be one of the better explanations, it is plausible, and shouldn't be discounted entirely.

Sethite View

- Sons of God = 100 percent human
- Nephilim = 100 percent human

The Sethite view is probably the second-most-popular view. It appeals to the context of Genesis 5, just before the mention of the sons of God and Nephilim. So it has good support regarding the literary context.

One variant of the Sethite view is that the sons of God were kings or rulers. This has some biblical support, such as Psalm 82:1–6. Also, this would explain why many ancient cultures refer to demigods as well. It also explains how ancestor worship can arise, even in a post-Flood realm. But both of these Sethite views still have their problems.

In both of these Sethite views, it is assumed that there was a godly lineage from Adam to Seth and followed down the line to Noah:

Adam–Seth–Enosh–Kenan–Mahalalel–Jared–Enoch–Methuselah–Lamech–Noah

In this godly lineage of Sethites, they were called sons of God in the context of the previous chapter. These sons of God (or their children) married or began marrying ungodly women (daughters of men), and their children followed after false gods and rejected the one true God. In other words, they fell away from God — recall the word Nephilim is related to the verb series "to fall" in Hebrew. In this view, offspring from these unions had fallen from God and were termed Nephilim.

Commenting on Genesis in *Exposition of Genesis*, H.C. Leupold was one of the leading commentators to promote the view that Nephilim were Sethites.[92] However, there are still a few problems with equating godly Sethites and Nephilim. Were these men and their descendants all godly? Of all of Adam's children, Seth was deemed worthy to replace Abel, who was righteous, and with him, people began to call on the name of Lord (Genesis 4:26). Enoch was indeed godly without a doubt. In the genealogy listed in Genesis 5, Enoch is singled out with honors unlike any other from Adam to Noah and ascended without death. Noah was righteous among his generation and found favor with the Lord (Genesis 6:8–9).

Were other Sethites godly? Perhaps several in the patriarchal list were righteous, but probably not all Sethite descendants, which is one of the biggest arguments against this view. It seems that there would have to be some godly heritage passed along for Noah to have any teachings to remain righteous when others weren't. However, we need to keep in mind the great ages of these patriarchs. Noah lived 950 years, Seth lived 912 years, and Methuselah lived 969 years (Genesis 5). So a godly heritage could have been passed from Seth directly to one of his descendants, such as Enoch or Methuselah, and then directly to Noah! (Many Bible scholars assume that Methuselah was also godly since his father Enoch, who walked with God in an incredible faith, would not have erred by failing to pass on a godly heritage to his son — Genesis 5:24; Hebrews 11:5; Jude 14.)

The patriarchs in the lineage from Seth to Noah's father Lamech died prior to the Flood, which was a judgment on man's sin, so they avoided this judgment. Was this because they were all godly? Perhaps. Regardless, this doesn't give any solid biblical evidence that confirms that the others in the lineage were righteous and godly.

If we look at the descendants of some of these others in the Sethite lineage, why didn't they pass a godly heritage to their children? Remember that the other sons and daughters of Methuselah (Genesis 5:26) and Lamech (Genesis 5:30) did not make it to the ark, and unless they died before the Flood, they would have been considered wicked (Genesis 6:5). In light of this, many Sethites were not saved from the Flood but perished, indicating Sethites weren't necessarily godly and shouldn't all be lumped together as sons of God. This is why some hold to merely the kingly or direct line of Seth to Noah as godly.

Another problem presents itself for the Sethite view when we discuss Numbers 13. Post-Flood, everyone was a Sethite! Where did *those* Nephilim come from?

There is another inconsistency with this view. Genesis 6:1 uses the term *men* to refer to mankind in general, and then in verse 2, *men* (daughters of men) is, in this view, inconsistently held as daughters of the Cainites. In all, this view has fewer problems than the previous one, but is still speculative in some areas.

Fallen Men View

- Sons of God = 100 percent human
- Nephilim = 100 percent human

This view is similar to the Sethite view, and it could be considered an "upgrade" to it as well. In this view, not all of Seth's descendants are assumed to be godly, but some of them were godly. This view also eliminates any perceived problem of the Nephilim in Numbers 13 needing to be Sethites, as there have been godly men both pre-Flood and post-Flood. It also holds consistency between the use of *men* in verse 1 and verse 2 of Genesis 6, keeping both as mankind.

In this view, *godly* men, such as some of the men listed in the Bible from Seth's line (perhaps some on other lineages as well), were called "sons of God" in keeping with literary context. So sons of God were merely godly men of the time.

Like the Sethite view, godly men (sons of God) were marrying women who were not godly (daughters of men), such as Cain's (or others of Adam's) descendants, including ungodly people from Seth's line, thus resulting in Nephilim because they *fell* away from God's favor. Once again, the Hebrew word *Nephilim* is related to the verb series "to fall." For example, we know Cain fell away, and Lamech (descendant of Cain) and many other men and women had fallen away. The Nephilim could easily have been people who had fallen or turned from God in a severe way. This would also make sense as to why some of Canaan's descendants (descendants of Anak were Canaanites) were called Nephilim in Numbers 13.

If you recall, Sodom and Gomorrah were so sinful that they were destroyed with direct intervention by God (sending the angels in Genesis 18:20, 19:24). This reminds us of the Flood — God Himself had a direct hand in destroying the wicked (Genesis 6:13, 17). When Sodom and Gomorrah were destroyed, it is logical to assume that many descendants of those people who were not living in the area any longer were not destroyed. In fact, the Bible doesn't say that all of the *descendants* of these places were completely destroyed. Therefore, it is logical that there could have been descendants living out away from the plain, such as Hebron, which is where the Anakites came from (Joshua 15:13).

The Bible indicates that the Anakites were descendants of the Nephilim, but it couldn't have been those wiped out in the Flood, since God destroyed *all* land-dwelling flesh. Therefore, it had to be a group of people that were *post-Flood*. If the Nephilim had fallen so far pre-Flood that God Himself destroyed the earth as a result of their sin, then it makes sense that the post-Flood account of a similar but smaller-scale destruction in Sodom and Gomorrah may well have been of the Nephilim. So the Anakites, who were Canaanites like those in Sodom and Gomorrah, very well may have been their descendants.

The sinners who died in the Flood and the sinners in Sodom and Gomorrah had one significant thing in common — they were the ones in history to fall so far from God that God Himself had a direct hand in destroying them. So it makes sense why these two groups could both be called Nephilim in this view: 100 percent human descendants of Adam who were in a state of having fallen far from God. Of course, there should be no dogmatism on this point.

What about the Book of Enoch?

The Book of Enoch is an ancient book that is attributed to Enoch, who is listed in the lineage from Seth to Noah. The Book of Enoch, Jewish traditions, and Josephus hold strongly to the idea that the sons of God were fallen angels and the Nephilim were offspring of such unions.[93] Even the Jewish translators of the Septuagint, who were known to make errors, translated the Genesis 6 phrase as "angels of God," revealing their beliefs. The Book of Enoch discusses in chapters 6 and 7 that fallen angels had relations with women. However, Paul and Christ warn us about Jewish tradition, and we need to keep in mind that the Book of Enoch is not the Word of God, but the words of fallible man (Titus 1:13–14; Mark 7:8–13;

Colossians 2:8). What this passage and the Septuagint do tell us is that people of those days believed the sons of God to be fallen angels.

It is true that Jude 14–15 quotes from the Book of Enoch (1:9). But that simply means that the quote used by Jude was inspired of God as Scripture. It gives no credence that any other verse in the Book of Enoch is inspired.

So is the book we have today really from pre-Flood Enoch? It wasn't enough to make the Canon of Scripture — it mentions Mt. Sinai, which shouldn't have existed until after the Flood, and Enoch lived long before the Flood. Rarely, if ever, do prophetic works reveal the future name of a place.

"Men of Renown" and "Men of Old"

Do the phrases "men of renown" and "men of old" mean they were the result of a special union?

Being renowned is simply having fame or being well known. Some Israelites were also men of renown (Numbers 16:1–2; Ezekiel 23:22–23). So saying that men of renown were offspring of special unions may not be wise.

Being "of old" comes from the Hebrew word *owlam*, which means *of long duration*, from antiquity, *ancient*, or literally *old*. It can also mean *forever* or *everlasting*. Of course, this makes sense since many of the patriarchs lived for 900 years (early, pre-Flood factors allowing them to live long ages[94]). God may have pointed this out to us for a significant reason — they were sinning for a long time!

They were likely making a name for themselves in wickedness (*renown*) and had been for a long time with no apparent end in sight (*of old*). This very well could have been the final factor to send the Flood to destroy them for their sin. It also lets us know that although they made a great name for themselves, it was no longer remembered due to God's judgment; not one of their names is remembered — we simply know them by the name *Nephilim*, which, as we've seen, is difficult to define even today!

Conclusion

Many respected Christians have commented on this topic over the years, and their work is to be highly regarded. This discussion is not to impugn their work in any way, but to build on it in an iron-sharpening-iron fashion (see Proverbs 27:17). In fact, their research has provided great insights into what I now personally believe about the sons of God and the Nephilim, and I commend them for their work.

As a ministry, Answers in Genesis does not officially take a specific stand regarding these four major views. It is not crucial to biblical authority, since each of the sides in this debate, for the most part, is using the Bible as the authority to make their case.

After researching this in more detail than anticipated, I was challenged on many occasions and affirm that this last view, the fallen men view (a modified Sethite view), may be the best at this point in my studies. However, there may still be problems that I have not had presented to me so far. As a fallible human being, dealing with precious little information regarding the Sons of God and the Nephilim, I may be wrong, but when I am wrong this does not in any way affect the accuracy of God and His Word.

In fact, there may be problems (or other views) that simply have not been brought to my attention. Regardless, I reiterate that Answers in Genesis doesn't officially take a particular stand on this issue as a ministry but seeks to encourage readers to carefully study the Scriptures and always maintain the Word of God as the ultimate authority on all things.

Endnotes

1. Just under 100 popular questions about creation and evolution and closely related topics are answered in the *New Answers Book* series by Master Books, Green Forest, Arkansas.

2. The term "man" in this context refers to mankind as a whole, which is commonly and simply called "man" in the Bible but refers to both men and women. Throughout this book, the term "man" is often used for the human race in general. It is not meant in any derogatory or chauvinistic sense, though sometimes it simply means Adam, the first man. So keep this in mind when reading the context.

3. Bear in mind that I am answering these questions to the best of my ability while using the Bible as my absolute authority. If there is a discrepancy between the Bible and what I have written, then rest assured that I am the one in error, not the Holy Scriptures.

4. Justin Martyr, *Dialogue of Justin philosopher and Martyr with Trypho, a Jew*, chapter 103. The Pharisees are the bulls: the roaring lion is Herod or the devil — A.D. 156.

5. W. Hanna, editor, *Natural Theology*, Selected works of Thomas Chalmers, Volume 5 (Edinburgh, UK: Thomas Constable, 1857), p. 146. The only thing Chalmers basically states concerning the gap theory in these writings is, "The detailed history of creation in the first chapter of Genesis begins at the middle of the second verse."

6. For a more detailed analysis of the days of creation please see: Ken Ham, editor, *The New Answers Book 1*, chapter 8: "Could God Really Have Created Everything in Six Days?" (Green Forest, AR: Master Books, 2006).

7. For a more detailed analysis on gap theory, please see: Ham, *The New Answers Book 1*, chapter 5: "What About the Gap & Ruin-Reconstruction Theories?"

8. Whether mankind had this power after the Fall is not the topic of discussion in this section and has been an extensive debate within the Church for hundreds of years.

9. I personally lean toward the serpent being a beast of the field (not dogmatically), as I understand that it could simply be compared to them in the same way we can compare a bird to the beasts of the field.

10. This excludes motion by gliding such as flying squirrels. Such locomotion is only temporary for land animals, and they have other means of movement while on the land. Note that we do not include birds as "land animals" although they live and reproduce on land or in trees (this is due to the biblical distinction that birds were created on day 5 and not day 6).

11. Henry Morris, *The Genesis Record* (Grand Rapids, MI: Baker Book House, 1976), p. 108.

12. Ibid., p. 107–109.

13. John Gill, notes on Genesis 3:14, adapted from The Online Bible, Larry Pierce.

14. Matthew Henry, notes on Genesis 3:1 and 3:14, adapted from The Online Bible, Larry Pierce.

15. John Calvin, notes on Genesis 3:14, adapted from The Online Bible, Larry Pierce.

16. Adam Clarke, notes on Genesis 3:14, adapted from The Online Bible, Larry Pierce.

17. Leupold, notes on Genesis 3:14, adapted from The Online Bible, Larry Pierce.

18. Matthew Poole, notes on Genesis 3:14, adapted from The Online Bible, Larry Pierce.

19. John Trapp, notes on Genesis 3:14, adapted from The Online Bible, Larry Pierce.

20. Allen P. Ross, *Creation and Blessing: A Guide to the Study and Exposition of Genesis* (Grand Rapids, MI: Baker Book House, 1996), p. 145.

21. C.F. Keil and F. Delitzsch, *Commentary on the Old Testament*, Volume 1: The Pentateuch, trans. James Martin (Peabody, MA: Hendrickson, 1989, original in 1875), p. 99; http://www.answersingenesis.org/articles/2010/01/26/satan-the-fall-good-evil-did-serpent-have-legs - fnList_1_14#fnList_1_14.

22. Flavius Josephus, translated by William Whiston, in *The Works of Josephus*, Antiquities, I:1,50 (Peabody, MA: Hendrickson, 1987), p. 30.

23. Gordon Wenham, *Word Biblical Commentary*, #1: Genesis 1–15, (Dallas, TX: Word, 1987), p. 78–79.

24. Frank E. Gaebelein, editor, *The Expositor's Bible Commentary*, Volume 2, "Genesis," by John Sailhamer (Grand Rapids, MI: Zondervan, 1990), p. 55.

25. From several statements (in addition to the one above) made by Calvin, this is the impression of the author regarding Calvin's point of view, although it is not 100 percent clear that he believed the change to be *only* temporary.

26. There were no land-dwelling, air-breathing animal kinds extinct by the time of the Flood since representatives of *each* kind were aboard the ark (Genesis 6:19–20). If this were a particular serpent kind that went extinct, it would have been after the Flood.

27. This was prior to the outpouring/indwelling of the Holy Spirit for Christians, which does away with the possibility of demonic or satanic possession in Christians (1 Corinthians 6:19-20; Luke 11:21).

28. Martin Luther, edited by Jaroslav Pelikan, *Luther's Works*, Volume 1 (St. Louis, MO: Concordia Publishing House, 1958), p. 185.

29. John Gill, *John Gill's Exposition*, adapted from Online Bible, Larry Pierce, notes on Genesis 3:6.

30. Ibid., notes on Genesis 3:1.

31. John Calvin, Calvin's *Commentaries*, adapted from Online Bible, Larry Pierce, notes on Genesis 3:6.

32. Matthew Poole, *Matthew Poole's Commentary*, adapted from Online Bible, Larry Pierce, notes on Genesis 3:6.

33. John Trapp, *John Trapp Commentary*, adapted from Online Bible, Larry Pierce, notes on Genesis 3:6.

34. Morris, *The Genesis Record*, 36th printing, p. 114.

35. Regardless of whether God also gave her the command and it was simply not recorded (the command was originally given to Adam) or it was transmitted to her via Adam, she still did not get the quote quite right.

36. Did Eve sin before she ate by possibly misquoting God? What we do know is that the sin of eating had repercussions (Genesis 2:17), whereas other potential sins may not have had the same punishment or was simply not recorded (i.e., had they refused to be fruitful and multiply). Later in Scripture there are instances where God is strict about adding to or taking away from of His Word (e.g., Proverbs 30:6; Revelation 22:18) and falsely attributing something to God or something that was God's to someone else would be sin (e.g., Matthew 12:24–32). Consider that death was the primary punishment for sin. Perhaps thorns or increased sorrow in childbearing were tacked on (in part) for not being obedient in other instances (i.e., because you listened to the voice of your wife *and* ate per Genesis 3:17.)

37. In fact, it wouldn't have taken long for them to sew fig leaves together either. After they ate, felt ashamed, and put together fig leaf coverings, the serpent still hadn't gone far. The Lord was able to call down the curse on the serpent, which wasn't far off.

38. Christian scholars have wrestled with the exact process by which Adam's sin is passed on (this will be in an upcoming chapter). The two major views are the federal headship and seminal headship views. This raises issues that should be discussed in the future article and is beyond the scope of this article.

39. Deoxyribonucleic acid.

40. The impeccability v. peccability of Christ debate centers on whether or not He could have actually sinned, since He is God and God could not sin. Since He could not sin, could He have actually been tempted? Conservative Christians have given three different responses, although all agree that He did not sin.

Those holding the impeccability view (Latin *non posse peccare*) say that Christ could not have sinned, and thus was not even tempted, during the "temptations." Those holding the peccability view (*posse non peccare*), say that He could have sinned. A third view attempts to find middle ground and is based on Christ having both a human nature and a divine nature. This view says that in His human nature, He could have sinned, but in His divine nature, He could not.

41. Some have argued that Jesus received none of Mary's genetic material because there would be mutations in the DNA and if Jesus was the model of perfection, then he could not have received such things. However, if Jesus did not get genetic material from Mary, then he is not the seed of a woman (Genesis 3:15), nor the seed of Abraham (Acts 3:25) or David, etc. So Jesus *had* to inherit material from Mary. Whether the Holy Spirit corrected any mutations or not is not the focus of this response and would likely require too much speculation.

42. Michael Toddhunter, "Do Leaves Die?" *Answers* magazine, vol. 1, no. 2, October–December 2006, http://www.answersingenesis.org/articles/am/v1/n2/do-leaves-die.

43. Ken Ham, editor, *The New Answers Book 2*, "How Old Is the Earth?" by Bodie Hodge (Green Forest, AR: Master Books, 2008).

44. Ryan McClay, "Dino Dinner Hard to Swallow? A Preliminary Analysis," AiG–USA, January 21, 2005, http://www.answersingenesis.org/docs2005/0121dino_dinner.asp.

45. Ham, *The New Answers Book 1*.

46. From "In Memoriam" by Alfred Lord Tennyson, 1850.

47. M. Buchanan, "Wild, Wild Life," *Sydney Morning Herald*, March 24, 2003, The Guide, p. 6.

48. Y. Forterre et al., "How the Venus Flytrap Snaps," *Nature* 433(7024) (2005): 421–5, found online at www.nature.com/nature/journal/v433/n7024/abs/nature03185.html; "How a Venus Flytrap Snaps Up Its Victims," *New Scientist* (January 29, 2005), found online at www.newscientist.com/channel/life/mg18524845.900-how-a-venus-flytrap-snaps-up-its-victims.html.

49. C.A. Brebbia, editor, *Design and Nature III: Comparing Design in Nature with Science and Engineering*, Vol. 87 of *WIT Transactions on Ecology and the Environment*, "Biomimetics of Spider Silk Spinning Process," by G. De Luca and A.D. Rey (Southampton: WIT Press, 2006), p. 127–136; see also en.wikipedia.org/wiki/Spider_silk.

50. D. Catchpoole, "The Lion That Wouldn't Eat Meat," *Creation* 22(2) (March 2000):22–23.

51. H. Mayell, "Anaconda Expert Wades Barefoot in Venezuela's Swamps, *National Geographic News* (March 13, 2003); found online at http://news.nationalgeographic.com/news/2002/04/0430_020503_anacondaman.html.

52. S. Carlquist, "Ontogeny and Comparitive Anatomy of Thorns of Hawaiian Lobeliaceae," *American Journal of Botany* 49(4) (April 1962): 413–419.

53. *Nature Australia* 26(7) (Summer 1999–2000):5.

54. Ref. 5; D. Catchpoole, "The "Bird of Prey" That's Not," *Creation* 23(1) (December 2000):24–25.

55. J. MacArthur, "The Origin of Evil," message delivered at Grace Community Church, Panorama City, California, Tape Number GC 90-235, 2000, online at http://www.biblebb.com/files/MAC/90-235.htm.

56. Whether man retains this ability after sin has been an important matter of debate ever since, but is not for this discussion.

57. Although we cannot be certain that Cain's wife was his sister (it could have been a niece, etc.), either way, a brother or sister would have had to originally be married to have offspring if it were a niece, great niece, etc.

58. James Ussher, *The Annals of the World*, translated by Larry and Marion Pierce (Green Forest, AR: Master Books, 2003), p. 18.

59. Bodie Hodge, "Ancient Patriarch in Genesis," Answers in Genesis website, January 20, 2009, http://www.answersingenesis.org/articles/2009/01/20/ancient-patriarchs-in-genesis.

60. Ussher, *The Annals of the World*.

61. Floyd Nolan Jones, *Chronology of the Old Testament* (Green Forest, AR: Master Books, 2005).

62. Ibid.

63. Others reasons include gaps in the chronology based on the presences of an extra Cainan in Luke 3:36. But there are good reasons this should be left out. It is included in late copies of the Septuagint (LXX). But early copies of the LXX do not have it, so it was added later. The 18th-century Hebrew expert John Gill points out: "This Cainan is not mentioned by Moses in Genesis 11:12 nor has he ever appeared in any Hebrew copy of the Old Testament, nor in the Samaritan version, nor in the Targum; nor is he mentioned by Josephus, nor in 1 Chronicles 1:24 where the genealogy is repeated; nor is it in Beza's most ancient Greek copy of Luke: it indeed stands in the present copies of the Septuagint, but was not originally there; and therefore could not be taken by Luke from thence, but seems to be owing to some early negligent transcriber of Luke's Gospel, and since put into the Septuagint to give it authority: I say 'early,' because it is in many Greek copies, and in the Vulgate Latin, and all the Oriental versions, even in the Syriac, the oldest of them; but ought not to stand neither

in the text, nor in any version: for certain it is, there never was such a Cainan, the son of Arphaxad, for Salah was his son; and with him the next words should be connected."

64. "Biblical Chronogenealogies," *Technical Journal of Creation* 17(3) (December 2003):14–18.

65. When the KJV was translated, *replenish* meant "to fill" and not "to refill" as it does today.

66. We know they can mate because land animal kinds were to reproduce after the Flood, and they were to come to the ark in pairs — a male and its mate.

67. John Gill, notes on Genesis 2:9, adapted from the Online Bible.

68. While the Bible doesn't say this explicitly, so one can't be certain, such an inference does seem logical.

69. Because Noah took "all food which is eaten" on the ark, some trees/plants would have probably been preserved (via seeds, etc.) by means of the food that was taken on board the ark (Genesis 6:21).

70. We are not taking an official position on whether man is dichotomous (body and soul/spirit; where soul and spirit are merely interchangeable words of the same substance) or trichotomous (body, soul, and spirit; where each are truly separate and unique). This is a disputed issue among theologians and there doesn't seem to be a clear answer to it. Personally, I would lean toward a view that incorporates both in a unique way. The spirit would be a modified *aspect* of the soul, like a flip side of the same coin. There is one coin but two unique sides to it. In other words, our soul is specially fashioned with a spiritual aspect, like duality. So soul and spirit could almost be used interchangeably (being two parts to the same "coin"), which we find in Scripture (Luke 1:36–47). Yet soul and spirit could be seen as unique (two sides of the "coin"), which we also find in Scripture (1 Thessalonians 5:23; Hebrews 4:12). Of course, a thorough treatment of this subject would require much more than this short footnote.

71. In some cases in Scripture, spirit and soul are used almost interchangeably, but not always. This seems to indicate that the spiritual aspect may be a modified part of the soul, such as the flip side of coin; this is why human souls with a spiritual aspect (made in the image of God) are truly unique to the souls of animals (merely *nephesh chayyah*). Although this subject deserves a paper in its own right, it is not for the discussion here.

72. "Multiply" is the key term that many people get hung up on. They think of it like a math problem. Zero times anything equals zero, so it wouldn't make sense to say that no pain would be multiplied. But when we think of it in terms of "increase" (the term the NIV translation uses), then there's no problem here. Also, she may have experienced pain in between her sin and this pronouncement.

73. *The World Book Encyclopedia*, Volume 1 (Chicago, IL: World Book, Inc., 1990), p. 570.

74. Ken and Mally Ham and Dan Lietha, *A Is for Adam* (Green Forest, AR: Master Books, 1995).

75. Considering that Adam and Eve were preprogrammed with language and knowledge so that they could immediately converse with God, they may have known right from the start that the fruit was edible. Though, I would leave open the possibility that this was some of the knowledge that they didn't need; and hence, not programmed into them. After all, they did not possess all knowledge, like God does (Colossians 2:3).

76. This was more likely the evening to give time for Eve to see the fruit and reflect on it during daylight hours — also giving them time to fashion some clothes out of fig leaves with the sun providing light for such activities.

77. Nevertheless, death reigned from Adam to Moses, even over those who had not sinned according to the likeness of the transgression of Adam, who is a type of Him who was to come (Romans 5:14).

78. Tim Chaffey, *God and Cancer: Finding Hope in the Midst of Life's Trials* (KY: Tim Chaffey/Midwest Apologetics, 2009), p. 184–185.

79. See also John 1:1–3.

80. Ken Ham, "Two Histories of Death," *Creation* 24(1) (December, 2001):18–20.

81. Whether this is still the case has been up for debate for centuries and is not for discussion in this short article.

82. Bodie Hodge, "Feedback: Who Sinned First?" www.answersingenesis.org/articles/2008/03/14/feedback-first-sin.

83. See Hebrews 7:9–11 and 1 Corinthians 15:22.

84. See also Isaiah 7:14.

85. Mark Bird, "The Trinity," www.answersingenesis.org/articles/aid/v3/n1/the-trinity; Bodie Hodge, "God Is Triune," www.answersingenesis.org/articles/2008/02/20/god-is-triune.

86. See Matthew 10:28, 23:33, 25:41–46.

87. See also Mark 1:15; Luke 13:3–5; Acts 17:30.

88. Due to the volume of authors, theologians, commentaries, etc., that have been written about the sons of God and the Nephilim, I've opted to not reference each argument and counterargument in detail, or I would have had more references than text. I have found that many arguments were recapped many times over and decided to stick with the arguments as the basis for this discussion. A few references are given that were required, though.

89. John Gill, *Exposition of the Entire Bible*, notes on Jude 6 and 7, http://eword. gospelcom.net/comments/jude/gill/jude1.htm.

90. Ibid., commentary on Genesis 6:2; http://eword.gospelcom.net/comments/ genesis/gill/genesis6.htm.

91. Many hold that fallen angels are demons, and that may well be, but is not for discussion in this chapter.

92. H.C. Leupold, *Exposition of Genesis* (Grand Rapids, MI: Baker Book House, 1956).

93. Flavius Josephus, translated by William Whiston, *Complete Works*, chapter III of *Antiquity of the Jews* (Grand Rapid, MI: Kregel Publications, 1867), p. 27–28; Book of Enoch, chapters 6–7.

94. Ham, *The New Answers Book 2*, p. 129–137.

About the Author

Bodie attended Southern Illinois University at Carbondale (SIUC) and received a BS and MS (in 1996 and 1998 respectively) in mechanical engineering. His specialty was a subset of mechanical engineering based in advanced materials processing, particularly starting powders. He conducted research for his master's degree through a grant from Lockheed Martin and developed a *New Method of Production of Submicron Titanium Diboride*. The new process was able to make titanium diboride cheaper, faster, and with higher quality. This technology is essential for some nanotechnologies.

Bodie published two peer-reviewed articles (with his advisor) on the subjects:

R. Koc, C. Meng, and D.B. Hodge, "New Method for Synthesis of Metal Carbides, Nitrides, and Carbonitrides," *Annual Progress Report Advanced Industrial Materials Program*, 1998.

R. Koc and D.B. Hodge, "Production of TiB2 from a Precursor Containing Carbon Coated TiO2 and B4C," *Journal of Materials Science Letters*, 1999.

During his years at SIUC, Bodie continued his personal study of biblical apologetics and began teaching this topic to a junior high Sunday school class. While at SIUC, he was the president of one of the few Christian student organizations, Christians Unlimited, and was also an officer in the student chapter of the American Society of Mechanical Engineers.

After earning his master's degree, Bodie worked as a mechanical engineer for Grain Systems Incorporated, was a visiting instructor in mechanical engineering at SIUC, and worked as a test engineer through Aerotek Engineering for Caterpillar, Inc., in Peoria, Illinois, at the Peoria Proving Ground.

While working at Caterpillar, Bodie continued to teach apologetics to junior high and high school students. He did this until accepting a position with Answers in Genesis in 2003. Currently, Bodie is a speaker, writer, and researcher at Answers in Genesis and is a regular speaker in the Creation Museum Speaker Series.

Bodie and his wife, Renee, were married in 2004 and have three children.